*Dr. Mir takes the read*er on a voyage through culture, *philosophy, religion, folk customs, poetry, science and more – all in service of helping others through his own experience with cancer. This is a guide to understanding one's own pain in a larger context than can help provide meaning and solace to many.*

Barrie R. Cassileth, MS, PhD
Chief, Integrative Medicine Service
Memorial Sloan-Kettering Cancer Center

It was a very enjoyable and gratifying reading, especially your wonderful use of poetic writing with deep spiritual thinking. It is also this insight into the spiritual part of a man's psyche and your positive outlook in life, even in difficult times that makes your work such a pleasure. It will no doubt be as rewarding to others as it has been to me.

Pia Maly Sundgren, MD, PhD
University of Michigan Health System
Department of Radiology

An inspiring celebration of life and journey into a mystic land.

Christina Bird
Author of Neither East Nor West N.Y.

In Secret Memories, *Dr. Mahmood Mir expounds both his syncretic spiritual philosophy and his recommendations for healthy living. Charming vignettes of his family's life in the Iran of the Shahs are interspersed with moral and health advice for the reader. The latter is the more pointed because it comes from a practicing surgeon who has had a "second career" as a long-term cancer survivor. Dr. Mir's generous, pacific, and inclusionary spirit pervades this work, and the reader is left wishing that the proud legacy of Persian history were left to people like Dr. Mir, rather than its current, unworthy inheritors. I am grateful for the opportunity of reading* Secret Memories.

Bard C. Cosman, M.D., M.P.H., F.A.C.S.,F.A.S.C.R.S.
Associate Professor of Clinical Surgery
Colon and Rectal Surgery

Anyone with a history of cancer or a family member with a diagnosis of malignancy, will greatly benefit from reading the wisdom contained in this book.

Tony P. Lopez, M.D.
Professor of Medicine
UCSD School of Medicine

Secret Memories
Spiritual Life

FOR

COLLEEN SANDUSKY

"WHEN YOUR THOUGHT IS A ROSE

YOU ARE A ROSE GARDEN "

[signature]

FEBRUARY 2. 2007

Secret Memories
Spiritual Life

Mahmood Mir, M.D.

Copyright © 2006 by Mahmood Mir, M.D.

All rights reserved. No part of this book may be used or reproduced in any manner whatsoever without written permission of the author.

Printed in the United States of America.

ISBN 10: 1-59571-133-3
ISBN 13: 978-1-59571-133-5
Library of Congress Control Number: 2006926760

Word Association Publishers
205 5th Avenue
Tarentum, PA 15084
www.wordassociation.com

To our ancestors

Our children

Our grandchildren

Arianne, Alissa, Andrew, Adam

Alexander, Christopher

And their children to be....

Acknowledgements

I would like to express my gratitude to several professionals and colleagues for their words of wisdom and input which I deeply appreciate. However, I would like to express a special thanks and acknowledgement to the following for their unique contributions and insights.

Dr. Eugene Braunwald, a distinguished Hersey Professor of Medicine at Brigham Women's Hospital, Harvard Medical School, for allowing me to use the conclusion of his lecture "Cardiology: Past, Present, and Future."

Dr. Bard Cosman, Associate Professor of Clinical Surgery, and Colon and Rectal Surgery at the University of California San Diego for reviewing *Secret Memories, Spiritual Life,* and for his sincere comments as well as thoughtful remarks. After reviewing this book, he so eloquently remarked "Dr. Mahmood Mir expounds both his syncretic spiritual philosophy and his recommendations for healthy living."

Dr. Tony Lopez, Chief of Internal Medicine at the University of California San Diego for reviewing this book and his kind words which has inspired me to continue forward in expressing my experiences.

Dr. Pia Maly Sundgren, PhD, Associate Professor, Department of Radiology at the University of Michigan for her constructive criticism, which gave me with further insight into the complexity of the editing process.

I also appreciate the blessings and kind words received from Christina Bird, author of Neither East Nor West who stated that this book was "an inspiring celebration of life and journey into the mystic land."

These acknowledgements could not be complete without a special thanks to Dr. Barrie R. Cassileth, Chief Integrative Medicine Service, at the Memorial Sloan-Kettering Cancer Center in New York for reviewing this book and providing kind words which are nutrients for the mind, body and soul. Dr. Cassileth wrote such an eloquent summary that I feel compelled to quote it in its entirety: "Dr. Mir takes the reader on an extraordinary voyage through culture, philosophy, religion, folk customs, poetry, science and more-all in the service of helping others through his own experience with cancer. This is a guide to understanding one's own pain in a larger context that can help provide meaning and solace to many."

Acknowledgements and Author's Notes

Since a good portion of this book was written during late hours while bed ridden during many sleepless nights, I would like to give special thanks to my wife and partner of life, Beverley. This book would not have been possible without her patience and love. She has contributed the most through her perseverance, by typing and re-typing multiple chapter revisions and maintaining her serenity despite my multiple demands. Thus, I truly thank her from the bottom of my heart for being a so kind.

I would also like to express my thanks to our children: Miriam, Suzette, Kevin and Halleh for their loving support and presence. Furthermore, I thank my brothers, Ali, Darooish, and their families, many nieces and nephews for their support as well as continuous inspiration.

I also owe sincere appreciation and thanks to Marlys and Andrew Schrag for the extra time and contributions in editing and proof reading my many revisions of this book. My deep gratitude goes also to my son in law, Per Rålamb for all his efforts in coordinating the logistics and providing the expertise necessary in publishing this work.

Thanks to Shahir Kharvari for his outstanding work of organizing the current Khavari's genealogy and to Melisa Laux for her wonderful illustrations. I thank the nurses, church members, family and friends for their prayers and blessing throughout this journey. Finally, I would like to thank my patients for trusting in me. I have learned through them many lessons of life and gained profound insight into myself and the complexities of the human spirit. Through these experiences, insights and contributions resulting in my spiritual growth – I share my journey with you in my story of life.

Table of Contents

I Human Life, Day One and the Day After — 21

Sun Worshiping in the Past	23
Celebrate the end of life with your love ones rather than being sad	24
Twenty First Century Man, Are we alone?	25
Human Body	25
War of the nerves and endocrine response	27
Immune system	28
The role of genetic in human life	29
Loving and giving	30

II Different land, different culture, and different language (Farsi) — 32

Adventurous Merchant	33
Governor position and hostage taking	35
My three daughters	36
The English translator	37
My life	37
Adventure	38
Balance	39
Choices with challenges	40
Drug-free life	40
Four months later	41
Education	42
Family	44
God	45
House in Shiraz	46

Our house in Tehran	47
Stories behind the house in Tehran	49
The gun	50
Majlis (Parliament) and the neighborhood	50
Independence	51
Journeys	53
Unclaimed Honey	54
Kindness	54
Kind or Kill	55
Romance	55
"I am going to kill you"	56
What happen to Buick?	57
Marriage	58
What happen to the bricks?	59
World War II with the Iranian Railroad (1939-1945)	59
Tehran Conference	61
A devoted human being	62
Zoroastra	63
Persian Empire	63
Related Historical sites to see in Iran	64
Poem of Love	66

III Persian Life and Customs — 67

Time to celebrate	68
Norouz	69
Food for the growing mind "ash"	72

IV Book of Life (our blueprint) — 75

Human genome — 75
Stem Cell, Self Renewing Cells — 78
Cancer prevention — 79
Healthy Living — 83

V Discover a Healthy Lifestyle — 85

Hypertension — 86
Heart — 86
Does fruit and vegetables intake protect us against cancer? — 88
Alternative therapy in cancer pain — 89

VI One Should Not Fear The Word Cancer — 91

VII Have A Sense of Humor — 96

Today is not the day — 97

VIII Alternative Therapy — 100

Some of the complications related to therapies — 102
Herbs — 103
Red wine, alcohol and medicine — 105
Aspirin in Medicine — 108

IX Body and Soul — 110

Summary — 110
Higher Self — 111
Where do I come from? — 113
Spoken name after life — 113
The ancient Egyptian concept of the soul — 114

Spirit	114
What is soul?	114
Native American spirituality	115
Ancient Persian religion	115
Universal energy	116
Out of body experience	116

X Art of Converting the Inner Pain to Happiness — 119

Finding the root of pain or what makes us "happy"	120
Stress coping and health	122
Gift of life	123
"I do not have time to die"	123
Do we need each other?	124
Relationships	124
Why loneliness is hazardous to your health?	126
Rich in heart and mind	127
Achieving happiness	128
Path of Life	130

XI Seven Steps to Heaven — 131

Light	131
Life	132
Love	134
Learn	136
Land	138
Legacy	139
Lord	141
Lessons to remember	142

XII Sufism — 144

History of Sufism	144
The first famous Sufi woman	146
Sufi Orders of rituals and initiations	147
Colorful cloaks	148
Rules to follow	148
Sufi Codes... meanings	150
Mevlana Jalal u Ddin Rumi	151

XII History of People With Vision — 154

Mother Teresa	154
Gandhi-known as Mahatma	156
Albert Einstein	156
Madam Marie Curie	157
Joseph Lister	157
Sir Alexander Flemming	158
Ivan Petrovich Pavlov	159
Jonnas Edward Salk	159
Zakariya Razi	160
Ibu Sina, Avicenna	162
Louis Pasteur	163
Robert Koch	164
Florence Nightingale	
William Stewart Halsted	165

Future — 167

Preface

A thirteenth century Persian Sufi Master named "Rumi" said, "In everyone and everything there is something good, find it as you would search for a shiny pearl in the heart of a shell." I call it in human terms the seed of knowledge or wisdom while scientists refer to it as DNA (deoxyribonucleic acid) which contains the genetic codes within our existence and passes our blue prints from one generation to another. The structure and format of future Life comes from our past or at least is influenced by it. Each one of us has many untold stories which we can share with each other.

As Rumi said "Let us open up the body's shell and free the inner light and energy to let it shine and glow as the Creator placed it in our heart and soul." With hope and understanding we can turn the negative energy to positive energy, the negative thought to a positive thought and promote the miracle of healing from within us, even in a case of a disease without borders like cancer.

I would like to give you guidance on how to cope with the condition and overcome the addictions with self-help and alternative therapy.

Remember the miracle of your own birth brought about by your father and mother.
Remember that your life follows the laws of nature; listen, visualize it and learn the secrets. Celebrate every happy occasion. Share it with your family and friends as frequently as possible.

Today is the first day of Spring in 2006. It is now over two years after my recovery from paralysis of the lower extremities and a near death experience, as well as 12 years since the diagnosis of Stage IV Cancer of the Prostate Gland with extensive bone metastasis. I celebrated my day by walking alone on the beach in Southern California. I am thankful to God to be alive and active, "as I am and the way I am" as quoted from Omar Khayyam. Enjoy the treasures of *now* at the present moment. I have many more stories to share with you as well as the gift of love and understanding. We can learn the exciting and challenging lessons of life by choosing a well balanced life style, physically, mentally, and spirituality with one step at a time. Let me take you on a trip to a different land with a different culture, different customs and a heart warming poetic language (Farsi) and mystic Sufism. Let us begin with "Life" and the life of a surgeon on the other side of the stethoscope.

Chapter 1

Human Life
Day One... And The Day After

*There was a door to which I found no key,
There was a screen past which I could not see,
Some talk a little while of me and thee
There seemed and then no more of you and me.
The secret of creation is behind the seen.*
Omar Khayyam
12th century Astronomer, Poet of Persia

I was amazed by the logic of a ten-year old boy, who was being treated at the Mayo Clinic for malignant brain and abdominal tumors. His mother asked him, "Do you wish you could go back inside of my uterus for a new start in life?" His response was, "absolutely not! This world is a better place to be" and he continued to say when my time has finished here on the earth "I will accept my transition to another world with peace." I think this child was physically turning his negative energy into a positive energy. He was mentally converting negative thought to positive and he seemed capable spiritually of recognizing the reality of a higher state of mind and being.

My father died when I was young and in his final days he stated "I am dying." I answered him "You are not dying you are traveling from one world to another." Indeed at the end we transform our energy from one stage to another. Like stars we also come and go. Many stories have been told over the course of history of mankind. According to theological books and literature (Cambridge, Mass.), God created a man from mud and dust and called him ADAM (man) ADAMAH (Earth, and HAWAH which became EVE in Greek, EVE in English means the mother of all living. God breathed into man's nose to give him life, "Breath of Life" so became the basis for "Spirit" in the pure and God's like part of him.

Rumi stated, "Human asked God to revel himself. God's voice was heard and said, "Since I could not reveal myself to you, I made you a part of me, so when you see yourself, you see me within yourself. The Native American Pawnee Indians have a story about Mother Earth and the first man which goes as follows: The Mother Earth and the seed of the corn caused movement, Earth gave life. Life being given, we moved upward to the surface. We shall stand erect, as Man! The being became human, who became Man.

In the beginning and through the course of human civilization each human being saw the tree of life on Earth and returned to heaven in his or her own way. In my paper

I called it "Seven steps to Heaven" and talked about light, life, love, learning, legacy, land, and Lord. In certain regions of the Near East and Mesopotamia, four religions were started. Zoroastrinism (Old Persia), the religion of ethical dualism, "Good thought, good word, and good deed." Judaism is the discovery of one God in Nature and social processes. Christianity is the religion of Jesus with love and mercy. Islam is the interaction with various cultures. God, the creator and sustainer of the Universe, joins the spiritual hosts of good men and angels in forming a community of beings devoted through good and evil realization of God, rather than worshipping and sacrificing animals. Reference books Avesta, Torah, Bible, and Koran,

Sun Worshipping in the past

Sun rays in Egypt were used to treat illnesses. Akhetaten (horizon of Aten) in 1360 BC was dedicated to the worshipping of one God (sun god) and his name was changed to Akhenaten (service of Aten). Akhenaten was the father in law of King Tutankhaten. Ancient faith of Persia, the Aryans, respected the sun and fire as signs of purity as did the Zoroastrian and Hindus.

One of the most exciting mysteries known to man is how the solar system came into being. According to astronomer Gerald P. Kuiper (1950), the sun and all the planets were formed from a big ball of energy, a cloud of prominal gas. The star we live by is the sun. No other object in our galaxy is as important to man as the sun. The sun is a central fire upon which all life on the Earth depends on along with any other life that may exist in the world somewhere or in the solar system. Yet, if the immense energy released from the sun's core reached the surface all in the form of gamma waves, as it was originally created, the result would be a death ray spreading throughout the solar system. Fortunately, the rays are softened during their outward journey like filtration of human souls in their final stage of life.

Celebrate the end of life with your loved ones rather than being sad

Life on Earth is more than one's self and our three-dimensional world according to James Van Praagh, author of *Talking to Heaven*. Energy exists within us and in everything around us. Within our physical body is a spiritual body. During the stage of death, the spiritual body is released or freed from the physical body. The spiritual body does not bring any disease or sickness that afflicts the physical body. The spiritual body moves from point to point with liberty (some people may even have this spiritual movement while they sleep). When a person dies let them go free and celebrate that person's move to heaven. When you are holding them, by clinging to their spirit, they are held to this world.

As an individual, we are mortal but as generations of human kind may be immortal. We shine like the moon and stars as the result of sun power (genes) of our parents and this gene is passed on generation after generation. We are not only dependent in this world on each other but on our environment and the Universe as a unit. David Suzuki, a scientist and astronomer stated; "We are the earth through the plants and animals that nourish us. We are the rain and oceans that flow through our veins. We are the breath of the forest of the land and the plants of the seas. We are human animals related to all other life as descendents of the first born cell."

How can I possibly have come so far yet still so far to go?
Ashley Brilliant 1933

Twenty first Century Man, Are We Alone?

For most of human history the heavens were the domain of God or God's being who inhabited the kingdom beyond the Earth. Today scientists and governments are actively researching and listening for signs of life out in the Universe. In order to progress in the twenty first century, we have to explore the unknown but even more importantly to discover ourselves. Albert Einstein, a man who devoted his life to exploring the unknown, said in October 1930, "the most beautiful thing we can explore are the mysteries, it is the true source of all art and science."

Human Body

The human body can heal itself, physically, mentally, and spiritually, call it a miracle or a fact of biology. The truth about self-healing is the training and learning of how to interact with our mind. Using positive thoughts and energy instead of negative ones (as the ten-year old boy) you learn to live in a state of balance life and harmony with nature, choosing health over illness.

These are a few tips for self healing:
- Be in charge of <u>your</u> life.
- Have a positive attitude, relax and meditate daily.
- Reduce stress, control your emotions (*Don't sweat the small stuff*, by Richard Carlson, PhD.)
- Choose a healthy lifestyle, diet, and exercise. Eat five to nine servings of fruits and vegetables as recommended by the American Cancer Society, 2005. You may add antioxidants to your diet such as Beta carotene, Vitamin, A, C, E, Selenium, Omega 3 (fish) low red meat, low fat diet, etc.
- Avoid toxins (smoking, drugs, burned charcoal food).
- Use natural methods to treat common illnesses.
- Support your immune systems.
- Control your blood pressure by avoiding stress (war of the nerves).
- Maintain a normal healthy weight.
- Avoid refined sugar.
- Keep yourself happy since heaven and hell are within our existence, choose a healthy balanced life, physically, mentally, and spiritually.
- Keep your mind and body busy. Work hard and sleep well.

- Laugh and love are the essential nutrients for survival of the soul. "Love is an extension of self love to others. You cannot give something that you do not produce. The more you love, the more you have love."
- Do three good things for yourself and others daily. Good thought, good words, good deeds.
- You should make time for your faith and meditate daily.

War of the nerves and the endocrine response

Everyone has experienced a degree of fight or flight reaction, when the body is under threat, which has made the heart pound, the mouth get dry, the hair will stand up at the back of the neck and the eyes seemingly pop out of their sockets. This is all part of the "fight or flight" response by which the body prepares itself for a defense reaction.

The hypothalamus, pituitary gland, and the adrenal glands together facilitate survival from stress. For example: when stung by a bee or fire ant, our reaction to the venom may range from local pain and swelling to life threatening anaphylactic reactions. Mild to moderate signs and symptoms range in their manifestations from hives, itching with redness over the body to the more signs and symptoms of trouble breathing and the tongue swelling. The more severe reaction would include anaphylactic shock or a severe asthma attack with respiratory failure. Patients who experience systematic reactions can be placed on Allergen, an immuno-therapy, and vaccinated with a specific vaccine to help prevent these reactions.

These examples really are only the tip of a complex part of the human organism. Parallel reactions are the cases of repeated mental stress and chronic illness, the immune system is bombarded with negative thoughts and energy, which is harmful to the entire system. The good news is that most diseases are self- limited. However, we are faced with bad news daily in our lives and how we react to it along with our perception to the events can make the difference. Support your immune system. Choosing a healthy attitude is important for self-healing.

Immune System

By definition, the immune system is the integrated body of systems of organisms, tissues, cells (white blood cells) and the cell products such as antibodies that differentiate the self from non-self and then neutralizes potentially pathogenic organisms or substances as infections, bacteria, viruses, tumors, foreign proteins, and etc.

"As it takes two to make a quarrel," stated by Charlie Chaplain, it takes two to make a disease, the pathogen and the host. We have all in the shrine of our bodies, materials to overcome infection and diseases, so it is important to support and protect the immune system by first removing the cause, and second the alternate therapies.

Specific vaccines are under study for certain tumors such as M-Vac for melanoma in Australian clinical trials, leukemia vaccine at MD Anderson Medical Center in Texas and other centers. "What is new in the book of Life?" Researchers have been working to catalogue the identity and location of each of the estimated three billion chemical base pairs in the Human DNA at the National Institute of Health, *JAMA* July 19,2001/ Lancet, February 16,2005. Healthy living requires a well- balanced lifestyle. According to Psychologist Susan Blackmore, behaviors and ideas copied from person to person by imitation-mimes may have forced human genes to make us what we are today. Complex behaviors like clothing, hairstyles, cheering, language, cigarette smoking, religions, interventions, theories and so on. Scientific America, Oct. 2000. So blame your parents!

The Role of Genetic in Human Life

The role of genetic factors, in the causation of human diseases, is one of the most rapidly growing fields in medicine. Contrary to the common belief, many genetic diseases are far from rare and in fact are significant causes of the illness and mortality as with the life of the ten-year old boy at the beginning of this story.

Paradoxically, one of the most important benefits of identifying the genetic factors in disease susceptibility is the opportunity for prevention and treatment of the clinical disease by manipulating the environment of the individuals identified to be genetically at risk. Today the stem cell research is in progress. New England Journal of Medicine, 2005, Drs Douglas Kerr and John Gehart from John Hopkins and MD Anderson in Texas and other locations. Dr. Eric Olson of the University of Southern Texas is evaluating the fat from lipo-suction for the stem cell research.

Loving and Giving

Tell me how much you love me and I will tell you it is sufficient indeed. We may not always realize that everything we do affects not only our life, but touches our loved ones and others as well, so start today by having a helping hand, kind words, and sharing your love with others. I like this spiritual saying:

I shall pass through this world but once,
Any good things therefore that I can do,
Or any kindness that I can show to any fellow creature,
Let me do it now, let me not defer or neglect it,
For I shall not pass this way again.

Today is the Spring of 2006, here in San Diego, California and we are blessed with a heavy rain. I plan to go out later for my daily routine by walking along the beach and thanking God.

Here is a beautiful poem from Hafez, a well known Persian Poet, from 1390.

Spiritual Life

I am content with a single rose from the garden
I am content with the shadow of a cypress tree in the field
Oh God, help me to avoid the hypocrites of the world
From the wealth of the world a jug of wine is sufficient indeed
They promise paradise for good behavior
For me liberties and tavern will do indeed
Friends sit at the edge of the river and see how the water passes by
I got the message, this is our life and destiny to arrive indeed
See what is happening in the materialistic and cruel world
You may be interested, for me what I have is sufficient indeed
When my love is with me, nothing else I seek
Her presence makes me strong even though I am weak indeed
Hafez, be thankful to the Lord, don't grumble
Your delightful poetry is enchanting indeed.

Chapter II
Different Land, Different Culture, and Different Language (Farsi)

The future belongs to those who believe in the beauty of their dreams.
Eleanor Roosevelt

Life in the future is determined by the actions in our past. Deep within the molecules of each of our cells, God planted the seeds of wisdom, "DNA" which carries his energy and our genetic code. I pass this history down to my next generation so they may understand their past. Yes, it is genetic but it is also up to you the choices you make in your life. Think wisely! Remember the miracle of your birth, your mother, and your father! Remember your life follows the laws of nature! Listen, visualize it, and learn the secrets.

This chapter is a part of my personal history to share with the people who are most important to me. I have tried to express myself the best way I know how and hope you find something that touches you. What I have written is from my heart. My wish is that these words connect our generations in understanding each other.

Adventurous Merchant

Before I start my 1001 night's stories, let me describe where I come from.

My father, Mir Abootaleb was born in Kazeroon, state of Fars, Iran. He later moved to Shiraz and finally settled in Tehran. He traveled frequently and had a vast vision. He once said, "I brought you from Kazeroon to Shiraz, and from Shiraz to Tehran, from now on going to Europe or the U.S.A., you are on your own." With his guidance, my siblings and I found our way in the world and we respect his legacy and the lessons he taught us.

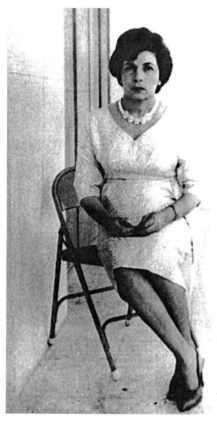

My mother, Shams Khavari was from a prominent family in Shiraz. [Refer to the genealogy of the Khavari family via Internet at *www.gencircles.com* or *rootsweb.com*.] My mother had a strong character which of course was necessary to raise five children, and she ruled with both a strong will and a generous heart. She lived a long, prosperous life and taught us the values of family, education and discipline. I have only the fondest memories and appreciation of my parents and dedicate this family history in their honor.

Governor Position and Hostage Taking

When my father was a young merchant with an office in Kazeroon, one of his family members was running for the Governor position. It was, however, a challenge because the opposing party candidate had more guns and power.

My father was taken hostage for a period of time. But, before any harm happened, one of his loyal workers, who ironically happened to be in a position of power in the opposing party, helped him escape. He gave my father a horse and proper clothing and guided him out of town in the middle of the night.

My father went to Shiraz, and with the help of friends and associates, and started all over again. He later moved on to the capital Tehran where he became a successful wholesale merchant mostly dealing with teas from Ceylon, and India. He also exported cotton and imported cloth from England, gaslights from Japan and other merchandise from the United States.

He became a commissioner and was elected many times as President of the Merchants between Shiraz and Tehran. His success was due in part to his personality – he had many friends and associates who trusted and liked him.

My Three Daughters

In addition to having eight sons, my father had three daughters that he was very proud of. In their honor, he named his tea company, "My Three Daughters." The code name for his company was "Bentley" although it's a mystery to the family what the code was used for, and his cable code was "Mir Tehran," which shows his status in Tehran at the time.

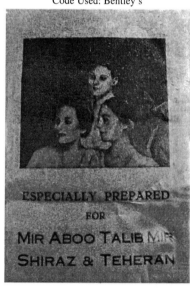

Cable Add: Mir

MIR ABOOTALEB MIR
Sirous Avenue,
TEHERAN
Importer, Exporter & Commissioner
Code Used: Bentley's

No._____
Date_____

The English Translator

There's a story of an English translator who worked at our father's company who was quite a cheater. Once my father received a number of bills from an American tire company (I believe B.F. Goodrich), which made no sense to anyone in the office since they did not deal in tires. Upon investigation, it was discovered that the translator was importing tires from the U.S. and charging them to the Company. The man was selling the tires on the side and pocketing the money. However, the young man was married to my father's niece so out of the goodness of his heart, my father forgave him.

My Life

It gives me great pleasure to share my personal life journey with you the reader, friends, and family and especially to pass it on to my grandchildren. It is like the story of 1001 Nights, if I start now, it may take 1001 nights to finish it.

Now that I am living with advanced cancer, I have many sleepless nights with a wandering mind scanning through windows and skylights and waiting for the morning sun to shine. I questioned in my mind, "what can I do?" The answer was easy. I created a game starting from A to Z tapping in the library of my mind for positive events and places that I've visited throughout my many years.

I thought I would share my beautiful dreams, fantasies and sweet and sour experiences. These true stories are part of my legacy that I leave behind.

A – Adventures in my life
B – Balance
C – Choices that I made with challenges to face, including mistakes that I made.
D – Drug-free life which relates to my recent experience with morphine therapy and the difficult withdrawal which I will discuss in detail later.

I had a hard time with Z since I could not learn adequately from zebra so I zoomed to the Old Persian religion of Zoroastrian with the doctrine of "good thoughts, good words and good deeds." Let us unravel these mysteries of life one by one and it's then up to your imagination to fill in the blanks that may have been omitted.

A – Adventure

I have vivid memories of my early school years in Tehran. I remember taking a field trip to "Shemiran," a beautiful resort area north of Tehran and toward the Alborz Mountains (front cover photo). It's a city of natural beauty with many small waterfalls, gardens, and lush plants and fruit trees. General Schwartkof, in his autobiography, he expressed many good memories of Shemiran while at the age of 10-11 when he lived and went to school in Tehran. His father was an organizer for "Amniyeh," a branch of the military task force under the power of Reza Shah.

Anyway, during my field trip I climbed up a solid, rocky mountain to the middle of a cliff and reached a point where I could go neither forward nor backward. Needless to say, I was shaking like a leaf upon this realization and shouted for help. My coach, who fortunately heard my voice, came to my rescue and led me back down.

I later in life climbed that same cliff again just to prove to myself that I could and it was a great accomplishment for me. When I reached the mountaintop it was amazing – the air was so fresh, the rocks covered in snow and what a beautiful view. It was such a wonderful feeling – I felt like an astronaut taking his first step on the moon. It was 1969 and Neil Armstrong made history by becoming the first man to walk on the moon and uttering the immortal phrase, "one small step for man one giant step for mankind."

B - Balance

From my earliest memories I was interested in a well-balanced life and harmony with Mother Nature. I was very close to my family and friends and enjoyed playing but I always made time for my schoolwork. During high school, I played sports including short distance running, jumping and disc throwing with some success. I won 2 medals in one year while living in Tehran. There is a Persian proverb as such, "a healthy mind lives in a healthy body" which translates into many cultures as mind and body connection or yin and yang.

C - Choices with Challenges

Our family foundation was based on love, discipline and truth. We were well coached and I didn't have any problems with certain restrictions in my life. We were guided as a group to make good choices and by doing so our life had a purpose without too much confusion. As the psychologist, Dr. Abraham Maslow said over 50 years ago "by choices that we make for purposeful living, we can live the highest quality of life that humanity can offer." In other words, when you make right choices early in your life that inspiration and purpose later on becomes part of your life.

D - Drug-free Life

Two years ago in mid-January 2004, I was placed on multiple pain medications starting with low dose Fentanil patch (narcotic) which they soon increased and then onto stronger narcotics. I was given a morphine I.V. in the emergency room followed by a period of long-acting morphine by mouth both morning and evening and short-acting morphine in between. I was under the care of hospice and other physicians. I needed more and more medications.

As the result of anemia and continuous morphine intake, I had shortness of breath requiring oxygen therapy throughout the night and periodically during the day. The narcotic side effects were staggering – I had uncontrollable vertigo, dizziness, chest pain, breathing problems and I was unable to eat, sleep or walk. I was completely bed-ridden. Not to mention severe constipation, angina pectoris (chest pain) and unresponsive to sublingual nitroglycerine and again had to go by ambulance to the emergency room. However, there was no evidence of coronary artery disease as was tested earlier by stress tests and coronary angiography. To make the story short, I was actually dying during the month of February and my entire family showed up to say goodbye.

I was neither dead nor alive – in a state of agony. One morning, right or wrong, I decided to stop all the medications including the morphine. It was difficult but for me it was possible, tolerating 7-10 days of withdrawal symptoms, which was worse than the addiction. One cannot but wonder why some people start such dangerous drugs without medical illness. Lord only knows!

Four Months Later

I originally thought God had sent me a non-stop ticket from earth to heaven but came to realize that God has a sense of humor. He stopped at the North and South Poles as well as many other places. As Billy Graham said, "all the planes that go to heaven, they stop in Atlanta."

After discontinuing the morphine and starting an alternate medication, I moved from the bed to couch, to the recliner, to the wheelchair, to the walker, then one day I found I could walk around the house unassisted. I am thankful to the Lord and with the help of my loving wife and children, I am back in action. I am going out in the world and started to live again. Suffice to say, at the time of this writing it has been many months that I haven't taken a single pain medication, not even Tylenol or aspirin. Call me anything that you may... With faith in God and self-determination, you can do anything that seems impossible.

The 13th century Persian poet and philosopher Sadi said, "every breath that we inhale is a breath of life and when we exhale, it is the freedom of the spirit. Every act requires being thankful to God and every moment is a time to be cherished."

E - Education

Education is the number one priority in my family. Sadi, a Persian poet and philosopher over 700 years ago said the following; "A philosopher told his children, dear to me as life, acquire knowledge for there is no reliance that can be placed on worthy possessions, either of land or money. You cannot take the land with you, silver and gold has its occasional risks, by either a thief carrying it off in one swoop or the owner spending it. But the knowledge is an ever spring fountain, a source of enduring health and if an accomplished person can not be wealthy, it matters not for his knowledge, his wealth is existing in his mind and is also an asset for the society."

My father had 11 children total, six from his first wife, Rogeieh, and five from my mother, Shams. His first wife died as the result of childbirth complications. My oldest brother, Mohamad-Reza, followed the path of our father and became a merchant. The next son, M.T. Mir became a famous surgeon, he trained in Tehran and the University of Colorado and was a Professor of Surgery at the University of Shiraz. He was the author of many books including *Surgical Technique* and *Surgical Diagnosis*. My oldest sister, Soadat, became an educator and Professor of Literature in Tehran. This was quite impressive because at that time only a handful of female professors existed in Iran. My middle sister, Shariat (Sheri) became a midwife working at a large hospital in the city of Ray (the old capitol and birthplace of Razi, a famous physician over 1000 years ago). Sheri also had an office in Tehran close to home. My brother Hassan became a lawyer and judge handling many good positions. My brother Hossein served in the police force as a Colonel and he also had a law degree, which helped him to obtain better positions in his profession. My third sister, Ghamar became an educator as well and later took a degree in Radiology in Chicago, Illinois and she already had a degree in art.

I became a surgeon and trained in general surgery in Chicago and New York. I held teaching positions at the Cancer Institute at the University of Tehran and the VA Medical Center in Dayton, Ohio. Afterwards I settled in Ohio to raise my family and worked in private practice for many decades until my retirement to San Diego. My brother, M.K. Manoochehr had a childhood injury but nevertheless owned a few shops near our house in Tehran and supervised the shops.

My brother, Ali is a pediatrician still enjoying his active, well-known practice in Wisconsin. My youngest brother, Don (Darioosh) is an engineer, who held many prominent positions in both Iran and the United States. At the time of the Shah's regime, he was President of Dorman Diesel in Tabriz and in California he was President of Catipellar Tractor Industries.

My nieces and nephews also followed the advice of their parents and grandparents and many became professionals as well. We have doctors, dentists, psychologists, pharmacists, therapists, teachers and many other types of professionals in the first and second generations. Thanks to good genes and good motivation.

F - Family

Can you imagine 11 brothers and sisters, 5 nieces and nephews – a brand new bride and groom living together at one time or another under the same roof? We ate together, played together and even had friendly fights together. Such a vivid memory of childhood and we remain a very close knit family to this day.

I will also talk about our houses in Shiraz and Tehran further ahead. In the meantime, we had on the average, 3-5 servants working in the household – a cook, a maid, a man in charge of buying supplies and taking care of the yard. Sometimes a nanny when the kids they were small. My father also had an assistant to drive him to the office and back. The household was always very busy with regular visiting guests on a daily basis, which was also enjoyable with lots of hugs and kisses free of charge. But, we had hiding places despite the large crowd for occasional privacy and meditation.

G – God

By loving and respecting each other, we have God's energy in our heart, home, body and soul on a daily basis. As Victor Hugo wrote, "to love another person is to see the face of God." There is one God for all of mankind. Joseph Campbell told a story about local jungle natives in the rain forest, he said, "a native once said to a missionary, your God keeps himself shut up in a house as if he is old and infirm, ours is in the forest, and in the fields and on the mountain, when the rain comes, I hear his voice." Are we talking about the same God?

During my early days, when I wanted to talk to God, I took the back stairway of our house in Tehran which went to the rooftop. The fresh air and beautiful view was enlightening, and the shining stars and the moon were witnesses of my visitation. I enjoyed every moment of it. Even today as I talk or write about it, those moments are still very vivid and enjoyable.

H - House in Shiraz

As I recall, our house in Shiraz was located near the bazaar. It was constructed of two adjoining houses connected at the center, exit at two lanes, covering the entire block. The front house, which was larger was at the north side was three stories, all surrounded with plenty of space, each sections had its own stairway and small hallways. The Northside section had a central large room with multiple large stain glass windows (for both sun protection and decorative effect), and at one corner a small spiral stairway going to a single room on the third floor which was my father's office. These became my hiding places where I watched the people passing by.

There was at the center of the yard a long multi-purpose pool which was always full of water with the flower paths on the sides and a large palm tree at one corner. At the central section connecting the two houses was a large kitchen, storage room and a place for drinking water with filters. At the top of the section was multiple rooms, including one called (Khayat-Khaneh) means sewing room with a Singer sewing machine for the talented ladies of the house to use. The second house was smaller with three sides and a two-story building.

Who was living in these houses? As I mentioned earlier, practically the entire extended family was living together. While my parents, brothers, sisters, nieces and nephews lived in the first house, my father's family was stationed in the second.

My grandmother's name was "Bibi," she was a beautiful and kind person. Then there was my uncle Mir-Nabi and Aunt Soghra. She was a very kind mentor. My father also had five sisters. One of these sisters who I remember very well married to a merchant in India, Azodi, and later moved to Shiraz and Tehran. She was also a very kind and wonderful human being. M.T. Mir went to University of Tehran Medical School and only visited during summer vacations.

I do have wonderful recollections from my early childhood at the age of 4-plus with my brother M.T. Mir. One night on the way back with my father and family members from a dinner party, I saw a pile of watermelon built up like a mountain at the bazaar. When we arrived home, I stated that I wanted watermelon and M.T. Mir carried me in his arms with the help of a servant back to the bazzar. We woke up the shopkeeper in order to bring home a few watermelons. They were then dropped in the pool and they floated. That was enough to satisfy my thirst. God bless their souls for their love and giving.

Our House in Tehran

The house in Tehran was a "home" not only to the family, relatives and friends; it was also home or a stop over to some migrating birds and ducks passing through from north to south. It had separate sections but was connected by walkways and hallways. The front yard was large and beautiful, full of shade, fruit trees and flowers. There were four large old elm trees covered with climbing vines at the south side or entry. One tree was without vines because us kids would climb and hide in it. In the middle was space made like a chair to sit on. At the center of the yard was a round pool with a fountain in the center with plenty of running underground water to use.

There were 4 gardens around the pool with a variety of fruit trees including apple, apricot, plums, persimmon, peach and a few more. We had many rose bushes and other seasonal flowers. The main building was a two-story structure with large central enclosed balconies. The upper one was fancy with plaster and elevated carvings, moldings and inlaid mirrors. It looked like sparkling stars with a beautiful central chandelier.

However, the balcony suffered major damage after an earthquake in Tehran and the repair work did not leave the same appearance to the balcony and the central guestroom behind it. The rooms were relatively large with high ceilings.

Long and wide hallways connected the first building to the second courtyard with stairways on both sides and one stairway in the front. The second courtyard, however, was smaller with a two story building (a maid's quarters) with plenty of storage room, kitchen facilities, underground water storage, and other facilities. Behind the building on the first floor were shower section and storage rooms.

The place had a touch of "Gajar" dynasty (the previous kingdom before Pahlavi or Reza-Shah). There were many tiles on the doorways and blue tiles stored by the wall of the second courtyard but they were never used.

Stories Behind the House in Tehran

Caring and sharing was a solid principle in our home. We used to eat our breakfast and dinner outdoors on the balcony during the summer months or in the courtyard. My mother "Shamsalzoha" served tea from a "samovar." The top contained the small teapot and the bottom the hot water heated by oil and fire. She was kind enough to peel homegrown apples from the yard and served one by one each person with love.

We had during my pre teen years a few Rose and Plymouth chickens, and a beautiful Persian rooster which was held in a designated area of the back yard. One morning the rooster got loose. He jumped on to the breakfast table and took an entire block of Persian cheese, which had been prepared for the morning meal for others members of the family. You can imagine the amount of explaining I had to do, yet I saved the life of my rooster.

During the summer months we slept outdoors on wooden beds and I remember, with some excitement at the time, waking up with the sudden drops of a brief summer rain shower and running indoors in the middle of the night.

Another vivid memory was my father would make his rounds late in the evening, kiss each child and all his grandchildren one by one before going to bed himself. I can still after all these years feel the touch of those delightful kisses on my cheek.

The Gun

In the Tehran house were four corner gardens with large elm trees surrounding cement pool filled with water in the center of the courtyard. In one of the corner garden while digging the center area, a wooden box was found. Inside the box was an old rifle and a few destroyed items but no money. It was known that at the time of Reza Shah owning a gun was illegal and so the gun was discarded silently by dropping it in a deep well without a trace of evidence.

What happened to the Tehran house?

My mother, sister, Ghamar, and brother Manochehr remained in the home years after the death of my father (near the Parliament or Majlis) until the late 1980's. They later moved to Shemiran (a northern suburb.) The house was sold and the new owner demolished the house and beautiful courtyard in order to build a six unit condominiums for profit.

Majlis (Parliament) and the Neighborhood

Majlis was about a fifteen minute walking distance from our house. It was almost always a center of multiple government activities. We were able to see the royal carriages and the guards passing by. The square, "Baharestan," in front of the Parliament was at times used for other activities as well as demonstrations. But, the neighborhood was in general quite safe and stable.

At the top of our lane was the home of a doctor with two boys who we grew up and played together with. Another neighbor in the lane next door was a holy man with a large indoor room (with a church like atmosphere). He had a prayer gathering with dinner open to the public once a week. Our home was number 3. Next door lived a couple with one daughter. The gentleman was a former Consulate General of Iran in Baku (Western Shore of Caspian Sea Area). Next door to him lived a wealthy businessman who had multiple grown children and the house next to him occupied by an Army officer. House number seven a gentleman working for Iranian customs office and the eight house coming back to the top of the lane were occupied by two teachers, one of foreign languages and the other of education. The relationship between the neighbors was quite friendly.

Independence

I always had the intention to be self sufficient in my life. Freedom meant detachment, detachment meant to be self-sufficient. Self-sufficient meant to have the tools and training for one self. We all have the resources and energy within ourselves. All we have to do is turn the thought process on and do the action. Dr. Wayne Dyer wrote "Say to yourself I am here on purpose. I can accomplish anything I desire. I can do it by being in harmony with the pervading creative forces in the universe." This will become a habit for life. Act as if anything you desire is already here. Use your inner energy and spirit to give you a uplift to success and inner peace will follow, rather than having a confused mind with wondering thoughts which we may experience one time or another. There are many ways to be independent.

I was sharing a bedroom when I was young with my brother "Hossein." As soon as Hossein worked and received his first lump sum salary he exchanged his paper money to solid gold coins. He placed the coins in a large bowl and brought out his treasure once a day. He would play with the coins under and over his hand and shake the coins. He would then place the bowl back in his closet and lock the door. His assets were safe with me and the family maid named "Akhtar" who was like a member of the family and well respected with love. We also had a watch dog named "Jeelah" to guard outside in the courtyard.

I believe my brother was looking for his first step towards financial independence. Hossein and I opened a business together. We had one room in a small building in the backyard and with an 8-millimeter movie projector and some movies like Charlie Chaplin. We sold tickets, candy, and made a small profit. Tickets were sold to family members and neighborhood kids. Recently one of the cousins from Dallas, Texas telephoned and the discussion of our home movies in Iran was brought up. He joked "Could he have his money back for his ticket for the days when the projector was not working?" We laughed about the business.

Journeys

When I was young my father, Mir Abu Taleb used to occasionally take me along with him on his business trips. We traveled sometimes by Jeep, and other times Mac trucks. There was an understanding I would at least have one over night stay some place.

I can remember going from Tehran (North) to Shiraz (South) passing through winding mountainous roads with snow on the ground before we reached the "Abadeh" - a beautiful village. We stopped for the night at the top at a tea and coffeehouse or inn to rest. It was usually a warm place with multiple wooden single beds covered with Persian rugs and blankets to sit or rest on. The house specialty was usually abgosht soup, chelow kabob, chicken kabob, and home made Persian cheese and bread. The inn could on occasion run out of food when they had a lot of passengers due to bad weather. You took your chances!

My father once told me while he was traveling with a few friends and associates they became snowbound in one of these small inns for one week. The owner of the inn told my father and friends "today I am going to give you a sandwich that you have not had before." Guess what it was? He placed hard and dry old bread between the two fresh homemade bread pieces. He served the bread to extend what was available for everyone. Never the less, everyone enjoyed it without any meat.

Unclaimed Honey

Once on a bus trip (TBT Company) from Tehran going to the Southern City of "Isfahan" a funny thing happened on the way. A few passengers on the one side of the bus saw and smelled fresh honey coming down the window and some was coming in and dripping on their clothes. Naturally the bus driver was told and pulled the bus over to the side of the road in a safe area to park. The driver and his helper had loaded all the passengers' luggage on the bus roof previously before the trip. Now the driver and helper were looking for the source of honey on the bus roof. It turned out that some person had a metal closed container full of honey wrapped with a cloth as their luggage but without personal identification. The weather had been warm and rough road had loosened the top of the container and had tipped to one side leaking gradually. When passengers were asked, nobody claimed ownership of the container. Watch where you sit when on a bus, there is always a next time.

Kindness

Kindness is a partnership. If you are kind to someone you are kind to yourself. Mystically speaking, you cannot hurt another person without hurting yourself. Nor can you help another without helping yourself. You share the same source of energy with everyone and consequently you must begin to think and act in a way that affects your awareness of this principle.

Kind or Kill

When I was a teenager my uncle, the late General M. Khavari, took me on a deer hunting trip south of Shiraz in the state of Fars. We were about ten to twelve people including the hunting guides. For three or four days some of us walked while other were on horses passing through the neighboring mountains in order to force the deer to enter a narrow valley down below. A guide and I were huddled in the narrow opening of this valley, in a small natural hole with rifles pointed upward just waiting to shoot the deer as they entered the area. The moment of excitement arrived and one by one or two at a time the deer passed over our heads and scattered freely toward the open space. Not one shot from the rifles was heard because of our hidden position. I did not shoot the deer because I was too interested to see them. The Lord on that day was kind to the deer but the hunters were not happy with me. The hunters had one good size buck (male) deer, which was shot the day before to take home. Needless to say, I wasn't included on the next hunting trip.

Romance

During my high school years I attended a famous school in

Tehran called "Addib" which means knowledgeable. The school was located on a very colorful street named Lalezar (field of flowering tulips). We were a total of forty students in one class and we had many knowledgeable and caring teachers to guide us. One of my classmates was a Turkish gentleman named "Buick." He lived near our house in Baharestan. Buick had two cousins, the oldest girl who I will call her "Miss T." and the youngest girl was Marrous. Both girls were charming and beautiful.

We use to run into each other on a daily basis – whether intentionally or accidentally. "Miss T." used to give me the latest news journal and other publications and she sometimes brought them over to my house. The publications were returned with great appreciation after I had finished reading them. "Miss T." was beautiful, intelligent, and very mature. I was naïve, athletic and from a well-to-do family which is maybe why "Miss T's" mother encouraged our casual or friendly relationship. But, this friendship was not acceptable to Buick. It seemed he was in love with her. I left and moved to Shiraz for further education and "Miss T." continued to send me letters and journals. We continued to be good pen friends. However the story did not finished.

I am Going to Kill You

I returned from Shiraz to Tehran after a summer vacation. Buick wasted no time and called me. He wanted to see me immediately on a specific date, time and at a certain bus stop in the suburbs called Shemiran. By being naïve, I agreed to see him on his terms and on that specific day in question. I saw him waiting for me as soon as I had stepped off the bus. His was very cold and unfriendly. We walked uphill toward Darband about five miles or more toward the foot of the mountain. His was very harsh and filled with anger. He said, "I am going to kill you." And by the tone of his voice I knew he meant business. "You stole my girl from me and I have your letters in my pocket to prove it." I knew the situation was bad and I had a lot of explaining to do. I knew my relationship with "Miss T." was on the basis of science and not romance but Buick was not convinced. He kept repeating a Persian proverb, "It is from me to me" (An eagle was shot with a bow and arrow fell to the ground. When he looked at himself and saw a broken wing, he saw his own feather was used as an arrow to penetrate the wing.) Buick again kept repeating it over and over, "It is from me to me." He blamed himself for introducing his cousins to me. Why? Why? It took four hours of uphill walking and sweating without water or rest to assure Buick that I would not communicate with "Miss T." anymore and that may be the reason why I am alive today.

What happened to Buick?

Eleven years later, after I had finished my medical education and surgical training in the United States, I returned to Tehran. My fellow classmates from my class of Addib School gathered together once a month in what was known as the Oil Company Club for dinner. They all became professional and successful. I never saw Buick again. I heard he became a businessman with ownership of multiple grocery stores in Tehran. As for "Miss T", I don't know where or what she does but God bless her kind heart.

Marriage

I was delighted to have witnessed a few wedding celebrations in our home in Tehran. Marriage between members of the extended family, cousins, or even distant relatives was considered normal. These type of marriage seemed to last a lifetime with respect, love, and support of the whole family.

Our house had a capacity to hold one hundred fifty to two hundred people. The backyard cooking area held food staples and supplies. Food preparation and catering was done as needed. The main dishes were served in the front house. Traditional Persian music and dancing followed after the food had been served. Some of the brides and grooms stayed in our home after the marriage ceremony until the construction of their new homes had been completed.

It was our father's intention to build a house for each child starting with the eldest. The first two homes were constructed in Baharestan close to the Parliament (Majlis). They were red brick two and three story with solid construction of steel and concrete for the foundation. My two sisters and brothers along with their spouses built their own home and moved to the North side of Tehran, yet keeping in touch daily with everyone.

What happened to the bricks?

As with any new building, there are always some bricks remaining on the site. When the two new houses in Baharestan were completed the bricks were piled like a mountain in the front yard. My nephew and I were in charge of watching the building supplies at the construction site.

One day, two men came with a pick up and told us kids "Your father, at the bazaar, sent us to clean up the mess at this site and the remaining bricks. They had a phony paper to do their work. The two men filled the pick-up with bricks and made multiple trips until the area was clean. That night when my father came home, we told him about the men he sent for the bricks and clean up. He was surprised, but laughed about it. Needless to say, he had not sent anyone. The police later found the men, but they had already sold the bricks and used the money.

World War II with Iranian Railroad (1939-1945)

Before World War II, Tehran was the capital, a busy, beautiful, mysterious, and a well decorated city. At night it was like a jewel sparkling with colored lights, carnivals, fireworks, yet bursting to celebrate every occasion rich to our old traditions. These celebrations took place at the city central square called Toopkhaneh, which was named after the Nadar Shah's big gun. Tens of thousands of people were joining in the celebrations including my mother "Shams" whom was a regular participant to these events.

It was September 3, 1939 when Germany invaded Poland and Reza Shah recognized that World War II was a reality. Iran was caught in the middle, being the "crossroad" between Europe and Asia. The country was brought into the conflict with no choice; despite it proclaimed neutrality, which only lasted until the summer of 1941 when Germany marched into Russia. The British and the United States had to find a way to get the military supplies into Russia through either Turkey or Iran.

The presence of German engineers, industrialist, and other technical experts, who had previously, came to Iran for various job development programs, including the railroad and other major projects made Iran the better choice. Foreign forces dictated to Iran to expel the Germans despite its neutrality. Allies invaded Iran on August 25, 1941 from the North and South. I remember the cheap Russian airplanes bombing Tehran around the Parliament; which was located a few miles from our house. The sound of the bombing was bad though the damages were minor.

Twenty two days after the invasion on September 16, 1941 Reza Shah realized that his days of ruling was over and handed Iran over to his twenty two year old son Mohammed Reza Pahlavi, who became the Shah. Reza Shah departed to Johannesburg, South Africa where he lived until his death.

During World War II, life for the average Iranian was difficult though not as bad as the Europeans who were directly involved. Iran had a 400% inflation rate. The railroad and other transportation were controlled in order to move military supplies, drugs and food to Russia night and day from the Persian Gulf to the Russian borders.

My father lost large cargo units packed with tea and cotton at the Gulf port, which was damaged due sitting at the pier too long. Iran issued coupons to the public for food and supplies. There were daily hardships for the people. One coupon could pay for "silo bread", hard like a brick and tasted like pure sawdust. But, my father was not only supporting his immediate family at this time, but the extended families were also included in Tehran. A total of forty to fifty people at one time or another lived in his home. Our meals were mainly rice, dates and vegetables. My father decided in the end to send his children and my mother to Shiraz for over a year. Shiraz was 700 kilometers south which was far from the conflict.

Tehran Conference

In the autumn of 1943, Russia, England, and the United States soldiers were looking for German Espionage agents at the various Embassies. Franklin Deland Roosevelt, Stalin, and Sir Winston Churchill secretly met in Tehran for a four-day conference.

President Roosevelt talked to the young Shah for several hours and gave him the American support to stand up to Russia. After World War II in 1945, the allied governments stated they were for one government of Iran in their desire for the maintenance of independence and integrity of Iran. The United States, England and the Soviet Union were required to leave Iran within six months after the end of the war. But the communist "Democratic Republic "created and supported by the Red Army stayed on much longer in the state of Arzerbaijan until a later date. The Iranian people gradually started to rebuild their lives.

A Devoted Human Being

After the death of my father, my *second father*, and brother Dr. M. T. Mir (a surgeon) took all the boys who were under age to Shiraz where he sent us to school with care and love. I was fortunate to live with my brother, who had created a luxurious lifestyle with a large beautiful home in town. He owned a very large garden out of town where he had built two large pools, one for swimming and another for the water lilies. The garden had a vast variety of fruit trees; with a gardener who attended to plants and several garden buildings.

Dr. M. T. Mir had a full time chauffeur available for our use as well. He was a devoted father, brother, mentor, and my professor of surgery at the University of Shiraz. He not only taught me the art of medicine, he also taught me about life and the art of humanity. God rests his soul. I admired him deeply from my heart and soul.

One day I approached him (Dr. M. T.) and said that I wanted to repay him back for his kind generosity. "No, he said, what I did for you—you do it for the others." What he meant was, whatever he had done for us it was a gift from his heart without any expectations in returns.

Zoroastra

Old Persian religion with the concept one God for mankind; Zoroastrian is the dualism of good and evil or conflicts of forces between darkness and light. The Holy Book Avesta proves that the existence of the faith was about 1000 B. C. if not earlier. Ahuramazda "Lord of Wisdom" started in 570 B.C. with the expansion of the religion was recorded on cuneiform[1] documents. Many famous Greeks including Aristotle knew of the Persian teachings including Avestas' were circulated through out Greece. Their doctrine was good thought; good words and good deeds come from this faith.

---

[1] Henry Rawlinson deciphered cuneiform inscriptions. (1836-1847)

Persian Empire (530-330 BC) and the Zoroastrian Ideas

The Near East, Egypt, Mesopotamia, and including Babylon each sector had their own Gods for different occasions. Hundreds of Gods were worshipped in the Near East, such as the sun, moon, sky, earth, water, and others. With so many Gods conflicts arose as to whose God did what until Zoroastrian introduced the concept of one God for mankind.

The public as well as the Kings of East and West were influenced by this concept. Cyrus the Great, a Persian Achemenian King and founder of the first world empire, chose to follow this doctrine of "Good thought, good deeds and good words." Cyrus the Great created the first declaration of human rights. "Love, humanity, and liberty combine with three ideals which is; think good thoughts, do good deeds, use good words" spread throughout the world. In 539 BC, Cyrus the Great entered Babylon without any blood shed and many Babylonians welcomed the Persians with his smooth words spread about his goodness, tolerance and piety. Hebrews welcomed him for he freed 40,000 of their people.

> *Thus says the Lord to his anointed Cyrus,*
> *Whose right hand I have holden*
> *To subdue nations before him...*
> *I will go before thee and make the crooked places straight.*
> (Bible Isaiah 451:2)

Related Historical Sites to see in Iran

- Tomb of Cyrus the Great is in Pasargad (North of Shiraz, State of Fars)
- Tomb of Darooish the Great is in Perspolis (North of Shiraz)
- Zoroastrian fire Temples are in Isfahan and Yazed and other locations
- Fire is the symbol of purity and sacred to the Zoroastrians.

Dear Reader,

Now that you have read some of my life stories — What are yours?

Body, mind, and spirit are all components of a whole person. You can not treat one without the other.

To stop wondering thoughts, Rumi suggested the power of relaxation by focusing on priorities, one subject at a time. Omar Khayam and Dr. Andrew Weil suggest paying attention to your breath and are in the present moment.

Poem of Love

I will finish this chapter by one of my own poems about love.

Love is the start of creation
Love is stronger than wisdom
Love is health, wealth, family, friends, country, freedom
Love is stronger than the wind, louder than thunder
Love is tears and laughter
Love is caring, sharing and happiness
Love is a dream
Love is soul
Love is sun
Love is moon
Love is the Earth and Universe
Love is air and ocean
Love is mountains and rivers
Love is plants and flowers
Love is the sound of birds
Love is the gift of God
Love is the seed for recycling
Love is beginning
Love is the end

Chapter III

The Persian Life and Customs

Mr. Churchill said "I like the name of Persia better than Iran since it represents the rich cultural aspect of the country." The name was changed over sixty years ago at the time of Reza Shah.

In Chapter 2, I mentioned some of the aspects of the Persian life and customs the way I experienced it. Persia is an historical land, 8000 BC, the Agricultural Revolution made it possible for permanent settlements and the creation of a complex civilization. Iran is a large country with 1,680,000 square kilometers almost the size of Great Britain, France, Switzerland, Spain, and Italy combined or one sixth the size of the United States. Despite many wars and invasions Persia has kept its integrity in the course of history including the Farsi language.

The Bible mentions the name of Cyrus (King of Persia) and Darioush the Great, hence, they are well known to many people. However, the Zoroastrian faith which began about 1000 BC with the Doctrine of "Good thought, good words and good deeds" is less familiar. Few Americans have heard this saying. The good news are the fame of its poets like Sadi, Hafez, Omar Khayyam, and recently Sufi Master "Rumi" are becoming more and more internationally known which has lead to enlightenment. Yet, a limited number of Persian literatures have been translated into the English language except the medical text of Avicenna's and Razi (found in Canon of Medicine which means Laws of Medicine by Avicenna) and few others. To stimulate your spiritual thoughts I have included poetry, short stories and teachings by Mystic Sufi Masters. Sufisim brings to humanity the culture of mankind with love and compassion regardless of religion or country of origin. Rumi wrote, "When your thought is a rose, you are a rose garden."

Time to Celebrate

A twelfth century Persian Poet and astronomer Omar Khayyam once wrote, "Yesterday is gone and tomorrow is not here, so enjoy the present moment "NOW". Many works have been written since that time about his poetry and philosophy including one by Edward Fitzgerald as well as many Persian writers.

Eckhart Tolle in his recently published best selling book entitled *"The Power of Now,"* a guide to Spiritual enlightenment and is very similar to Khayyam's philosophy. I have had the pleasure of visiting the Khayyam Library and Memorial garden in Naishabur (Khorassan) on multiple occasions.

For me, this life journey and illness has allowed me insight to value the treasure of the present moment, and positively impacted my outlook on daily living. Spring of 2006 signifies two years following my recovery from paralysis of the lower extremities and near death experience. In addition, it is twelve years following my diagnosis of Stage IV Cancer of the Prostate Gland with extensive bone metastasis. I celebrate my days by walking alone or sometimes with my family and friends on the beach in Southern California. I am thankful to God to be alive and active as I am and the way I am. It is soon Norouz, the first day of Spring which is also the first day of the Iranian New Year, or New Day (Norouz). It was first celebrated by Jamshid, the King and the ancient Persian civilization.

Norouz

Norouz or New Day is perhaps the oldest Persian festival going back to mythological times. It has its origin in the calendar and the changing of the seasons. March 20 or 21 is this Vernal Equinox, the first day of spring when the length of day and night is equal. It is the time when the death of dormancy of winter is over and Earth begins to breathe a new life; a most appropriate time for the beginning of the New Year.

The ceremony is so old that different localities of Iran have their own traditions. However, there are certain customs that are observed all over. Norouz is a time of renewal, hope, and joy. Houses are cleaned for the occasion, new clothes are bought, gifts are exchanged and people pay visits to friends and family.

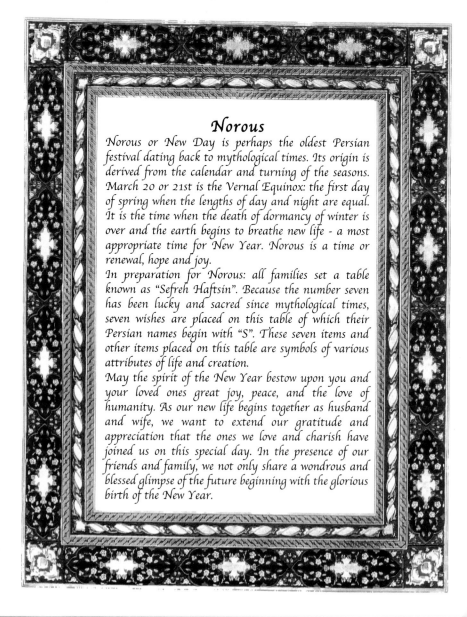

Norous

Norous or New Day is perhaps the oldest Persian festival dating back to mythological times. Its origin is derived from the calendar and turning of the seasons. March 20 or 21st is the Vernal Equinox: the first day of spring when the lengths of day and night are equal. It is the time when the death of dormancy of winter is over and the earth begins to breathe new life - a most appropriate time for New Year. Norous is a time or renewal, hope and joy.

In preparation for Norous: all families set a table known as "Sefreh Haftsin". Because the number seven has been lucky and sacred since mythological times, seven wishes are placed on this table of which their Persian names begin with "S". These seven items and other items placed on this table are symbols of various attributes of life and creation.

May the spirit of the New Year bestow upon you and your loved ones great joy, peace, and the love of humanity. As our new life begins together as husband and wife, we want to extend our gratitude and appreciation that the ones we love and charish have joined us on this special day. In the presence of our friends and family, we not only share a wondrous and blessed glimpse of the future beginning with the glorious birth of the New Year.

On the Wednesday evening before Norouz, known as Chaharshambeh Souri, people build small bonfires and jump over them shouting "may my paleness go to you and your glow come to me." The fire is a symbol of baptism. In ancient Persia, fire and water were two agents of purification. On that night we jump over the fire to be symbolically purified for Norouz.

In preparation for Norouz, all families set a table known as Sofreh Haftsin. Since the number seven has been lucky or sacred since mythological times, seven dishes are placed on this table of which their Persian names begin with "S". These seven dishes and other items on the Sofreh are symbolic of various attributes of life. These are *Seeb* (apple-beauty); *Seer* (garlic-health); *Sabzeh* (seed sprout-rebirth); *Serkeh* (vinegar-patience); *Sumagh* (sumac berries-joy); *Senjed* (fruit or service –happiness; *Samanoo (boiled malt with flour-prosperity)*. Originally, these represented creation. Some families add to the table, sombol (hyacinth); colored eggs for fertility (equal to the number of family members); a bowl with live gold fish (life and the sun changing from the constellation Pisces to Aries); a mirror (images of creation); candles (enlightenment and happiness); a bowl of water (purification) with gold and silver in it (prosperity); and according to the religion of the celebrant, a copy of the Avesta, Koran, Torah, Bible. Many add to the "Haftsin," a copy of poems of Hafez, one of the great Persian poets of the fourteenth century.

According to the calculation of astronomers, announced

many years before, the exact minute and second of the change of season is known. This occurs precisely the moment the sun crosses the equator. It is preferable that all members of the family gather around the table at this time to greet the New Year. In some localities, each member of the family dips his or her hand in the bowl of water and picks a few pieces of the gold and silver, jingle it and puts them back. The purpose is to be prosperous in the New Year but in an honest way. The water, the other agent of purification, purifies the fingers.

The last activity of Norouz is on the thirteenth day of the year. Since the number 13 is unlucky, the whole day or part of it should be spent outside of the house. This day is known as "Sizdeh bedar". It is a national picnic day. The Sabzeh (seed sprout) from the Norouz table, is grown tall by now and has received unto itself all the bad luck, is taken out and placed in a stream to be carried away, ending one year and going forth with the rebirth of another. "Good thought, good word, good deed, throughout the year"

Food for the Growing Mind "Ash"

A popular food in the Persian kitchen is Ash, meaning a special soup. Ash is a very thick tasty soup, which is believed to medicinal as well as nutritional qualities. The word for cook is Ash-Paz and the place that you cook is called Ash-Paz-Khaneh, translated literally as home of the cook. There are many varieties of Ash depending on the geographic location, the season, and the reason. However, the ritual is the same regardless of other factors. As one can see, Ash plays a very important role in the Persian home and is a favorite of all.

I remember during my childhood how Ash making was in our house a family affair. Everyone participated, grandparents, parents, children, the maid, and even the visiting guests. The ingredients of Ash includes, rice, grains, fresh vegetables, legumes, sometimes meat, fresh fruit, onions, nuts, pepper and other spices and usually a secret family ingredient. The ritual as well as the final product was very satisfying – a food for the body, mind, and soul. I will never forget the few hours that we spent together in preparation of Ash. We spoke of family history, told colorful stories and verses from the Koran, books about the Kings, Dervishes, Hajji-Baba, and we prayed. There was a lot of hugging, kissing, laughing, learning of traditions and respect for each other.

Today, as I look back on that time, I understand that it was not the stirring and taste of authentic tasty Ash which stayed in my mind, but the family unity, love, and caring which built up the immune mechanism and passing on the tradition with it. I've also learned in this country that the families that come together for traditional meals are closer, and often more loving as well.

In the gathering for a shared purpose, a bond is created. In the past, Persian families built their houses with a guest quarter, as is also done in some places in this country. Since there was no social security systems, families took care of the elderly who worked for them over the years by providing for the rest of their lives. Either the person lived in the guest- house, or in an elderly home facility, which was financed from one fifth of the family income (Khoms) which was provided for without question. Both of the women who worked for our family benefited from the general trust fund until they died.

Chapter IV
Book of Life (Our Blueprint)

God gave me a life
The value of every single day
He alone knows.
Rumi, 12th Century Persian Poet, Philosopher

Human Genome

Just as the second half of the twentieth century was the age of the computer, the first half of the twenty-first century promises to be the era of biology (Genome) and nature of diseases.

(MIT) Human life starts from one cell and the library of life is the brain of the cell. (DNA) The English word "cell" means "to hide." What is hiding is the secret of life. Our cell count is several hundred trillion and yet changing all the time. A unit cell is a complete machine. It makes, repairs, and renews itself. For example: the surface of our skin fall and rebuild every 60 seconds. The process of the disease or malignant transformation begins when the DNA of the genome is altered or damaged; in some way, oncogenic, abnormal mutation, viruses, radiation, toxins, chemicals, bacteria, and etc. However, gene alone does not produce cancer.

Gene	Somatic	Environment	DNA
Dysplasia	Mutation	Damage	Cancer

DNA mismatch during cell division can occur within three billion cells. Each could go wrong. Our body defense mechanism is the immune system fighting to overcome the pathogens. Genetic engineering strives to unlock the genetic secret of many diseases including cancer.

One day an infant born with a genetic defect of bone marrow or blood may be able to use his or her umbilical cord blood harvested at birth, repaired by engineering gene manipulation, and then re-infused into the body. Blood collected from the placenta and the umbilical cord, at birth contain enough stem cells that can replenish the blood and the immune systems of people with leukemia and other cancers.

Today, the stem cell research is in process. See (New England Journal of Medicine, April 2001/2005), Drs. Douglas Kerr and John Gehart at John Hopkins, in Maryland, MD Anderson in Texas and other centers. Dr Eric Olsen, (University of Southern Texas) is evaluating the fat from lipo-suction for stem cell research. Dr. Blake Cady in the (Journal of the American College of Surgeons, June

2001 and JAMA< June 2000) writes about newer advanced technology approach to genetic understanding by elegant alternative techniques.

Such as microarry analysis with molecular credentialing of cancer gene for the development of specific antibodies or alteration of gene, has opened up possibilities of specific control only imagined up to now. In simple language, in the future we can isolate specific gene or genes, which cause specific cancer as well as using specific medications to kill the cancer cells rather than killing good and bad cells with high toxic levels of the drugs.

Today, specific vaccines are under study for certain tumors such as M-Vac for melanoma: (Australian Clinical trials) leukemia vaccines at MD Anderson Medical Centers and so on. Researchers have been working to catalogue the identity and location of each of the estimated three billion chemical base pairs in the human DNA (National Institute of Health, JAMA June, 2000). There is human genome projects software to sequence chromosomes on the market for sale. For example, Heidelberg, Germany/United States/ Lion Corporation of Capetown, South Africa and two hundred fifty other research centers.

The future of finding the cause, prevention, and the specific treatment for cancer is bright. (Breast, thyroid, ovary, prostate, colon, rectum and so on) The laws of Mandelian genetics dictate that there is only a 50/50 chance of inheriting the familial predisposition to cancer. (25% free of disease, 25% will develop the cancer and 50% the carrier of the gene. Genetic testing for mutations in pro oncogene is now standard of care for children from families with multiple endocrine neoplasia, Type II, in part, this is because of the occult medullary thyroid carcinoma.

Key word: Genomic will change the nature of drug discoveries and treatments.

Stem Cells, Self Renewing Cells

Stem cells are throughout the body. The stem cells from the bone marrow and hematopoetic system have been studied extensively. Each cell line developing under influence of a specific humoral factor responsible for maturation and growth.(enzyme tyrosine kinase). At least, each cell can make one cell like the mother cell. Also, the adult nervous system contains resident population of stem cells. [1]Stem cell Research, Journal of American Cancer Society, March/April 2005. Just as some environmental factors can increase adult neurogensis, others can conversely alter the cell. Example: stress.

At the present time many medical centers in the United States are working on the *Biology of Genes*. These centers are: Sloan Kettering, New York, Salk Institute, La Jolla, California, University California Los Angeles, Los Angeles, California, Brian Druker, Oregan are just to name a few who identify, isolate, culture, turn over, pattern of individual cells, differentiation, and response to external injury and medications. Many drug companies are researching to unlock the genetic secrets of breast, colon cancers, diabetes, Alzheimer and etc. In testicular cancer a tiny pair of chromosomes could make a great difference in the life of Lance Armstrong and his son Brian for long term survival. (Bristol-Myers Squib Company, JAMA, 2000) The mutant cancer genes will be identified and repaired, even "switched off" in the near future.

Abnormal chromosome 22, and chromosome 9, and tyrosin kinase activity will cause the cell to bypass regulated growth and undergo malignant transformation to leukemia. (Chronic Myleogenous leukemia, JAMA, August 2000) Stem cell transplant to treat multiple myeloma is in the process by Adam Zaidi/David Vesole of Wisconsin. (Cancer Journal of American Cancer Society, September/October 2001.)

Cellular and humural immune dysfunctions in many cancers affect the growth factor and prevent apoptosis (cell death). Keyword: The biology avenues for the treatment of injury and illnesses are the gate for the twenty first century research.

Cancer Prevention

Is there a magic bullet for treating cancer? How near or how far away are we? First, let me stress that we do not need complex technology for simple solutions; but follow the common sense and guidelines by the American Cancer Society. Human beings are magnificently organized networks of energy, information, and intelligence in a dynamic exchange with the environment. Use your physical, mental, spiritual potential and discover the miraculous gift of creation that we are blessed with.

1. **Diet and Exercise:** according to the American Cancer Society guidelines on diet, nutrition and cancer prevention; reducing the risk of cancer with healthy food choices and physical activity. Eat five or more serving of fruits and vegetables, cereal, rice, pasta, beans, and so on, including dark bread and grain products in every meal. (Macro nutrient and micro nutrient)

2. **Limit your intake of high fatty foods:** particularly from animal sources. High fat diets have been associated with an increase in the risk of cancers of the colon, rectum, prostate, and endometrium. Eat small portions of meat (bake or broiled) instead of fried foods. Avoid saturated fat, eat fish and white meats instead of red meat. Fish is a good source of Omega three.

3. **Be physically active:** and maintain a healthy weight. Obesity increases the risk of colon and rectum, prostate, endometrial, breast and kidney cancers.

4. **Limit the consumption of alcoholic beverage:** if your drink at all. Oral and esophageal cancers are much more common in countries where alcohol consumption is high, combined with tobacco chewing and smoking.

5. **May use antioxidants:** many of the most common illnesses of our society are linked to free radical damage as in the cases of cancer, heart disease, stroke, diabetes, arthritis, osteoporosis, inflammatory bowel disease, glaucoma, retinal degeneration, Alzheimer's and early aging. A group of vitamins, minerals, and enzymes will protect the body from the formation of free radicals. (Atoms that can cause damage to the cells, such as radiation poisoning, toxins, chemicals and etc.) Antioxident (antioxidase) are the scavengers that are globbing up the free radicals. Useful antioxidents are the beta carotene, Vitamin A, E, C, minerals, selenium and etc.

6. **Avoid excess sun and radiation exposure.**

7. **Avoid tobacco products:** Lung cancer is the leading cause of death among Americans, more than eighty percent of lung cancer cases occur as a result of tobacco smoking. Chewing tobacco and snuff and alcohol single and together increase the risk of cancer of the mouth and esophagus. Eating recommended amounts of fruits and vegetables decrease the risk of cancer as published by the American Cancer Society.

8. **Yearly Check Up/Examination:** Skin, breast examination (mammogram), pap tests, colon and rectal examination, serum makers (PSA to detect prostate cancer) and so on, and thereby removing the pre invasive lesions of the skin and colon polyps.

9. **Immunization and Vaccination:** Immunization helps to eliminate a co carcogenic feature like Hepatiitis B infection to prevent hepato-cellular carcinoma (liver Cancer) vaccination and prevent sarcoma in Aid's patients.
   DNA tumor viruses:
   a. Epstein Barr virus causing Burkits lymphoma
   b. Herpes Virus causing cervical carcinoma
   c. Hepetitis B virus causing liver cancer
   d. Leukemia a retrovirus causing T-Cell lymphoma

10. **Antibiotics:** The use of antibiotics in the treatment of early gastric mucosa is associated with lymphoid tissue lymphoma and carcinoma resulting from infection with bacterial species helicobacter pylori.
    Treated with RX Prev Pac:
    a. Prevacid, 30 mg two capsules
    b. Biaxin, 500 mg two capsules
    c. Trimox amoxicillin, 500 mg 4 capsules
    Total of eight capsules a day for ten days

11. **Antiangiogenesis:** The use of antiangiogenesis compounds are to shut specific blood supply of tumors while leaving the blood supply to the normal functioning tissue. Theory of seed verses soil. Cancer cells, blood supply, and metastasis can be detected and hopefully eliminated. (B) Subpopulation metastsis (may lodge and grow) doubling time for breast cancer primary tumor of 1X1 centimeter may take as long as 25-30 years to grow. Metastasis to double may be rapid in 25-30 days.

12. **Protect your immune system:** The human body can heal itself physically, mentally, and spiritually. Call it a miracle or a fact of biology, the truth about self healing is the training and learning how to interact with our mind (stress reduction). Use positive thoughts and energy instead of negative ones. Learn to live in a state of balance with life and harmony in nature and the people around you, choose health over illness.

Healthy Living

This section has been mentioned twice because of it great importance.

Our body can heal itself physically, mentally, and spiritually, call it a miracle or fact of biology. Here are a few tips for self healing.

- Be in charge of your life.
- Have a positive attitude, relax, and meditate daily.
- Reduce stress. Control your emotions (*Don't sweat the small stuff* by Richard Carlson, PhD).
- Choose a healthy lifestyle, diet and exercise. Eat five or more servings of fruits and vegetables as recommended by the American Cancer society. You may add anti-oxidants to your diet such as beta carotene, Vitamin A, E, C, selenium, Omega 3 (fish), low red meat and a low fat diet.
- Avoid toxins such as smoking and alcohol.
- Use natural methods to treat common illnesses.

- Support your immune systems. Eat greens (parley, basil, herbs, spinach, kale etc.)
- Control your blood pressure by avoiding stress (war of the nerves)
- Maintain a normal healthy weight.
- Avoid refined or artificial sugars.
- Keep yourself happy since heaven and hell are within our existence, choose a healthy balanced lifestyle. Physically, mentally, and spiritually.
- Keep your mind and body busy. Work hard and sleep well.
- Laugh and love are key essential nutrients for survival of the soul. "Love is an extension of self love and to others. You must love and respect yourself, before you are able to love others. You cannot give something that you do not produce yourself. The more you love the more you have.
- Do three good things for yourself and others daily. Good thoughts, good words, good deeds.
- Make time for your faith and mediate daily.

If cancer has a genetic basis, why should I be concerned about nutrition and cancer prevention guidelines as recommended by the American Cancer Society?

The future of cancer therapy is bright, by using a specific medication for a specific condition.

Chapter V

Discover a Healthy Lifestyle

You save one life
You save the world.
Avicenna

"Nature does nothing without a purpose." Sometimes the greatest achievement, in life, is a simple life and lifestyle. The doctrine of the human self-healing has been, the foundation of the teachings of Hypocrites, Aristotle, Plato, Galen, Razi, Avicenna, and others.

Miguel Servetus, a sixteenth century physician and theologian wrote, "he who really understands what is involved in the breathing of man, has already sensed the breath of God" Sadi, a thirteenth century Persian philosopher, and poet, said "the first breath is the breath of life." Although the human body is complex but we can make our life easy by just listening to our inner voice. The human body is highly coordinated with various systems, including the immune system (defense system).
With a well balanced lifestyle, the human body can protect

itself against diseases both externally as well as internally: (bacteria, viruses, fungi, and cancer). When you select a healthy lifestyle you can overcome the stress of the daily modern life and its consequences. Such as high blood pressure, heart attacks, other stress related diseases. I will discuss a few common challenges that we are facing on a daily basis, including what is old and what is new, in the medical field today.

Hypertension is the most common reason for American adults to visit their physician today. More than 50 million people have elevated blood pressure which increases the risk of cardiovascular disease and stroke. Complementary therapies including diet, exercise, lifestyle modifications, and drugs as needed can help and prevent possible complications.

Heart (A Pump)

Greeks saw the heart as a forge burning impurities from the blood and soul. The Greek philosopher, Aristotle thought the heart is the first organ to live and the last to die. Leonardo De Vinci, a student of anatomy stated the heart spoke, if not volumes then closed to it, with what words will you describe the heart so not to fill a book. Rumi, a mystic, connected the heart to spiritual love, a living body, and the soul. Today, healthy living equals protecting your heart since coronary artery disease is the leading cause of mortality for men and women in the United States.

In a recent medical meeting in Anaheim, California (March 31, to April 2, 2005) Dr. Eugene Braunwald, Professor of Medicine at Harvard Medical School, also The living Nobel Prize winner in Medicine, stated in his discussion, the Cardiovascular aspect of the healthy living entitled *Cardiology, The Past, The Present and The Future.* He mentioned that since the discovery of circulation by William Harvey many more discoveries have been made in field of cardiovascular disease. Intervention verses prevention. Intervention such as electrocardiography, cardiac catherization, and coronary angiography, stent insertion, balloon dilatation, and echocardiography, placement of pacemaker, internal defibrillator and drug therapy, genetic intervention and many more.

Prevention is more rewarding especially with a large increase in the geriatric population high risk groups which include diabetes, obesity, family history of coronary artery disease and previous interventions need closer attention and care. The balance of prevention and intervention are more effective than a single treatment. Dr Braunwald concluded, in the future the principle role of the cardiologist will change from recognizing and managing the establish disease. As in the cases of today, interpreting and applying genetic information in prevention and treatment in 2020 and beyond. The grand goal of course is to eliminate cardiovascular disease as a major threat to long and productive life.

Does Fruit and vegetable intake protect us against cancer?

A recent study questions whether the long standing guidelines to eat 5-9 servings of fruit and vegetables can reduce the cancer risk may be overstated. In a report published in the Journal of the national Cancer Institute (2004), Walter Willett, M.D. and colleagues, at the Harvard School of Public Health, found that eating at least five servings of fruit and vegetables daily had an impact on cardiovascular disease risk but not overall of cancer incidence.

A National Nurse Study and the Health Professionals, follow-up survey, Willett and colleagues, examined the eating habits of 71,910 women and 37,725 men as determined by food frequency questionnaires. They compared fruit and vegetable intake with incidence of myocardial infarction, stroke, and all cancer combined (except skin cancer) or in situ breast cancer and organ confined prostate cancer. A study group who ate five servings of fruit and vegetables per day had significant reduction in cardiovascular disease risk, but overall cancer incidence was not affected by the amount of fruits and vegetables in the diet.

Author's conclusion "it is still possible that there may be a small benefit for cancer. "Discontinue smoking, avoid becoming overweight, and being active physically will be more effective in preventing cancer." The existing evidence does support the reduced risk for cardiovascular disease and is definitely stronger than all cancer combined.

Jeanne Calle, PhD, Director of Analytic Epidemiology of the American Cancer Society stated "When you eat fruits and vegetables you can meet your calorie need with healthy food, as opposed to meeting them with sugar, fat, or low nutrient foods." She additionally stated "making good food choices are going to directly protect you from heart disease."

Alternative Therapy in Cancer Pain

In chapter two, I mentioned that I was taking multiple pain medications including Vicodan – a narcotic combination. Narcotic medications are not only addictive but they also accumulate with a lot of side effects. I was taking one or two Vicoden tablets a day gradually increasing it to five or six tablets per day for over one year.

As a result of Codeine and other narcotic medications like morphine I reached to a point of non functioning stage (I hit a stone wall), which was an awakening for me. In a stage of agony to live or die, one morning I suddenly decided to stop everything. That day was Norouz, a new day, a new beginning. That was the time that my spiritual life took over and saved my life and soul. With self meditation and support of my family and friends I did overcome the disaster and survived with dignity. A simple foot massage, hot or cold packs were helping me without taking a single pain medication. Now I take two Tylenols once or twice a month that may be needed.

Chapter VI
One Should Not Fear the Word "Cancer"

A colleague of mine used to advise his patients who had been diagnosed with cancer that "Take your money from the bank and make a trip around the world, and live every moment of your life the way you want." To my knowledge, those that took his advice lived a longer and much happier life.

Even I followed his advice, last October when I made a trip to Connecticut and then Upper-State New York to a National Historical landmark. I was able to walk to the highest peak of the Mohonk Mountain area. I enjoyed the fresh air and the beauty of the trees with the autumn gold leaves with pleasure.

Diet and Cancer

Mahmood Mir M.D.

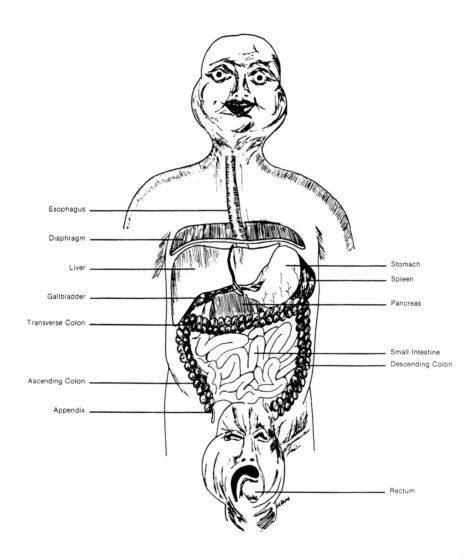

The following are a few examples:

Mrs. A is a thirty five year old professional woman, mother of two children, who was diagnosed with breast cancer and lower auxiliary (under the arm) lymph node metastasis. She underwent surgery, lumpectomy (removal of the tumor area which equates to about one fourth of the breast) with low auxiliary node dissection.

She then underwent radiotherapy and chemotherapy. Today, over eleven years after her initial diagnosis she is disease free, active, and enjoying life with her family.

Mr. D is a physician. At the age of fifty-five, he was diagnosed with hypertrophy of the prostate gland. He was treated by a (TUR) transurethral resection (shaving of the prostate gland.) The pathological report showed evidence of prostate cancer. No additional treatment was given except modification in lifestyle, diet, and exercise. Today, this physician is tumor free, over ten years after the initial diagnosis of prostate cancer. He is healthy and quite active.

Mr. S, this gentleman, at the age of sixty-five, was admitted to a hospital with acute abdominal pain, and distended abdomen. His initial diagnosis was gall bladder disease with partial large bowel obstruction (blocked bowel.) At the time of his surgery he was found to have colon cancer. He underwent a partial large bowel resection with end to end anastomosis (removal of the tumor and the surrounding areas with suturing of the two ends of the

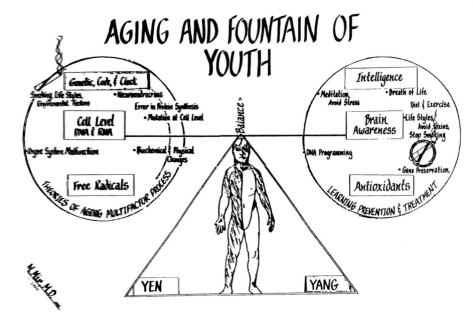

bowel together.) He has survived over twelve years, disease free with dignity.

There are numerous success stories, which I could mention, including a patient of mine, with five primary solid tumors and this is not including her skin cancer. She lived a normal life for over twenty five years after the initial diagnosis of her breast cancer.

In any event, if you are in a similar situation as I am, my advice is to focus on the most beautiful events in your life. Moments such as: a beautiful view, walking on a beach, walking through a flower garden, looking at the blue sky with white clouds. Rather than negative thoughts or events infuse your mind with positive ideas and thought to help the immune system. Our brain and nervous system are predisposed to damage through stress and bad news like cancer, yet we all have the power to heal that which we can.

By positive energy and making the right choices daily (smoke and drug free) we can have a better life. God always has a plan - all we need is vision and faith in our self and in God. When we bring spiritual practice into our personal life spontaneous healing will occur, as I experienced it. Sufi calls this event "spiritual enlightenment."

I remember the lovely Christmas songs that my children use to sing to me. "Do you see what I see?" which still echo's in my ears. Keep in mind that this has a profound meaning in our subconscious mind. For me I felt it in my heart and my soul. When you are in need, go back to your spiritual being, it will expand your vision, and help your immune system to overcome the problem or disease. Love and hope are your answers. Love for self and for mankind. One should not fear the name of "cancer."

Suggested reading books by Andrew Weil, M.D, called "*Spontaneous Healing,*" another book is Love, Medicine and Miracles by Bernie Siegal, M.D.

Chapter VII

Have a Sense of Humor

A few years ago, when I was admitted to a hospital for overnight observation, a young kind compassionate nurse entered my room and slapped my feet and said, "Welcome to the other side of the stethoscope." A little sense of humor and compassion will go a long way at the time of need.

During my practice in Ohio, I was surgically caring for the Catholic seminary and nunnery patients including a lovely and compassionate nun named Sister Mary. One evening I admitted a critically ill patient with a diagnosis of small bowel obstruction, which required emergency surgery. The nurses could not find a priest in the hospital anywhere, which the patient and his family had requested. I asked Sister Mary if she could help me in this situation since the patient and family were on the same floor. She responded "with pleasure." With the help of nurse and Sister Mary, who herself a patient, stood up from her bed and carried the intravenous pole and went to the patient in need, performed her holy prayers as required by the Catholic faith and returned to her room. Sister Mary's spiritual positive energy was enlightening for everyone around her. How powerful this event was. I will always remember her with great respect and dignity.

Today with the machine age, high technology has changed all aspects of our society and lives, some for the betterment on the other hand some for worse. This change is to such a degree that a sense of expressing our love and compassion has been diminished.

Stephen R. Covey (author of the *8 Habits of Highly Effective People*) said, "At the workplace we have reduced a person to a thing;" our mind, heart, and spirit are reduced to "a thing," which creates lack of trust. This statement is true about a wonderful patient of mine, Nancy; a mother of two children was diagnosed with breast cancer. She was traveling to a nearby clinic for chemotherapy and radiotherapy. She stated "sometimes when I am on the table they handle me like a piece of meat, not like a human being." Of course, that situation was corrected immediately.

Today is Not the Day

Two years ago, I went to a radiation oncologist for consultation. Shortly upon arrival the technician called me by name and I was told to "change in to this garment and climb upon the radiotherapy table." However I was sent over for a consultation, so I told the technician that "my astrological stars do not match with radiotherapy today." She laughed and went to let the Doctor know I was here.

When I refused the radiotherapy on that day and I was sent to the Doctors private office room. I was reminded of my early school age days going to the principle's office knowing that I was in trouble. In the office room the waiting time was relatively short. A well-educated knowledgeable Doctor walked in with my very thick manila chart under his arm and I could see in his face that he was not happy at all. My wife was with me for moral support and I knew I had to try and change the atmosphere now. So I thought I would mention a quotation from Dalai Lama. "Love and compassion are necessities, not luxuries, without them the humanity cannot survive." My radiologist responded in a monotone voice by stating "there is not such a thing as humanity." But knowing this Doctor I knew that he did not mean it and later we cooperated with each other to meet our goal.

As Mother Teresa said "few of us can do great things but all of us can do small things with love." On another occasion, I went to see my specialist physician for a follow up appointment. The specialist was suggesting certain medications for me and I was questioning the good effects as well as the side effects. Even to his knowledge the effectiveness of this injection was questionable and I therefore refused the injection. The good physician became upset to a degree that he told me "I am not going to do a rectal examination today," which was quite ok with me. However, the rectal examination in that specialty office was part of the routine order. I later mentioned the situation to another physician who knows my specialist very well and just laughed. The other physician said "you could tell the specialist to turn around and let me do the rectal examination on you" and we both had a good laugh.

Chapter VIII

Alternative Therapy

All that is written in books is worth much less than experience of a wise doctor.
Razi (842-932)

According to Dr. Deng and Dr. Cassileth from Sloan Kettering Cancer Center in New York, "Complementary therapy for pain, anxiety, and mood disturbances" is sometime as effective. Reported in the *Cancer Journal of the American Cancer Society Inc*, (2005). People with cancer commonly experience a range of symptoms including pain and various types of physical and mental distress. Drug therapy does not always adequately relieve these symptoms. Some people may not be able to tolerate their side effects of the prescription drugs.

Some patients may develop a tolerance to narcotics (Opioids), requiring increasing dosage of medication with accumulative complications. In this type of patient mind body techniques may be especially worth while as they may alter their perception of pain. Sometimes a foot massage could be beneficial. Also the National Comprehensive Cancer Network Guidelines is recommending consideration of non pharmacological modalities such as massage, acupuncture, imagery, hypnosis and relaxation training if the pain score remains four or above on a ten point pain scale. (0 means no pain—4-5 means moderate pain—9-10 means severe pain.)

Music therapy can also be beneficial in certain cases. Dr. Judy Orloff, a Psychiatrist from the University of California Los Angeles, author of *Power of Postive Energy* passionately believes that the future of medicine lines should include spirituality and our body subtle energy systems which is a vital part of our wisdom usually disenfranchised from healthcare." In her book, she guides you to intuitive healing and the steps towards developing positive beliefs about healing, listening to your body for sensing subtle energies, asking for inner guidance's and listening to your dreams.

Depression and chronic pain sometimes are tied to the type of procedure and disability that a patient experiences. As a result of surgery or other treatments, like chemotherapy or radiotherapy, in my case I developed severe gastrointestinal side effects which improved in time with conservative treatments.

Dr. Ian Kudel, PhD., Department of Psychiatry at John Hopkins University in Baltimore, Maryland reported at the annual meeting of the American Pain Society (2005). Dr.

Kudel reported a total of 279 patients were surveyed 1-4 years after mastectomy procedures. The prevalence of pain was higher (57%) than previously expected, with (22%) reported phantom breast pain. The survey was mailed to women who had undergone a mastectomy at John Hopkins at least one year earlier and the response was (56%.)

Dr. Kudel mentions that neuropathic pain can take up to six months to develop. Other therapies such as acupuncture's, mind and body techniques, hand therapy, and massage can relieve symptoms. I believe physical, mental and spiritual support with compassion and love are more effective in a patients care than medications and the use of high technology alone. It is absolutely necessary that the patient be part of the team work and the decision making (ask questions.)

Some of the complications related to the therapies

Non steroidal anti inflammatory drugs like NSAID, Bextra tablets, Celebrex capsules, Dolobid tablets, Naprosyn tablets, Feldene, Indocin capsules, Motrin IB tablets and capsules, Toradol and a few more surprisingly effective in the relief of arthritis as well as pain from metastasis bone disease. However, they are associated with gastro-intestinal bleeding (same as Aspirin) and may be associated with high blood pressure and cardiovascular problems. (JAMA April 2005, The Journal of American Medical Association.)

Both chronic pain and chronic opioid intake are associated with depression. One other complication related to therapy acupuncture needles are filiform sterile. Single use needles, despite aseptic technique, it is safer not to give acupuncture to patients with neutronpenia (low white blood count). Thrombocytopenia (low blood platelet count) or risk of endocarditic due to the heart valve abnormality yet not counting the cost and need for frequent visits to the acupuncturist.

Herbs

For people with long standing illness and established diagnosis of anxiety, or major depression; although the Pharmacologist intervention remains the most effective way of treatment, herbal medication can be used in the healing process. According to Dr. Deng and Dr. Cassileth and others, a handful of specific herbs are:

Available in the market:

Kava Kave:	used for anxiety, Ephedra (Mathurang) used for Asthma, stimulant, appetite suppressant
Valerian:	used as a sleep aid
St. John's Wort:	used for depression, seasonal affective disorder, anxiety
Passion Flower:	used in insomnia, anxiety, epilepsy, neuralgia, and Opiates or Benzodiazepine withdrawal

Ginkgo Bioba: used for dementia, peripheral vascular disorder, Sexual dysfunction and hearing loss.

Turmeric: (corcuma longa) another herb to mention is turmeric, a yellow color powder. This is used extensively in India, Egypt, and the Middle East for cooking as well as medical therapy. The roots and rhizome are used for inflammation, bursitis, arthritis, low back pain, skin rash, sore throat, menstrual pain.

Turmeric tea is used for dyspepsia (indigestion), gall bladder malfunction may improve bile production which is necessary for the fat digestion. Used as an anti inflammatory action, primarily is due to active substance Curcumin. Curumin is also anti histamine and antioxidant.

In the Middle East, turmeric combined with raw eggs and lamb fat, spread on a soft Bandage cloth is used for inflammation and wrapping (support) of a fracture site.(Cast) According to Amber Ackerson, N.D, curcumin is effective for cancer prevention and cancer therapy, along with metastasis combined with other treatments like chemotherapy and radiotherapy. Side effects with low dose, one to three grams orally per day, there is no known side effect. Caution should be with use of herbal medications and especially some of the dietary supplements.

Many botanicals contain biologically active substances that can effectively help in some ways beneficial yet may interfere with the effect of chemotherapy or surgery.

Consult with your doctor if you are on any herbal medications during the course therapies. For example, St. John's Wort treats mild and moderate depression but adversely changes the effect of the chemotherapy agents. Another word of caution, is drug interaction with any combined medications have been reported.

Red Wine, Alcohol and Medicine

Alcohol and wine have been part of human history, serving dietary and socio Religious functions for over more than six thousand years. Razi, a Persian physician and chemist produced alcohol for medical use over a thousand years ago; although he did not receive credit or recognition for it. Razi and Avicenna both used alcohol for wound irrigation and sterilization during this period. Avicenna stated "If you save one life, you save the world."

The cardiovasuclar protective effect of red wine

A recent study by Dr. Alfredo C. Cordova and his colleagues from Yale University, New Haven, Connecticut reported in *The Journal of American College of Surgeons* March 2005, has analyzed this subject in detail. Worldwide Program conducted by the World Health Organization

Researchers studied twenty one countries with over seven million men and women, from ages 35 to 64 years old.

From thirty-seven (mainly European countries) studies were taken over a ten-year period of time from 1980-1990. The investigators observed a lower mortality rate from coronary artery disease in France compared with that in England and the United States. Keep in mind other factors; like high consumption of saturated fats, and similar serum cholesterol concentrations, high blood pressure, and body mass index (individual weight).

Red wine prevents arteriosclerosis or hardening of the arteries although the condition is a multi factorial disease. Red wine may be a factor to benefit the reducing of mortality from heart attack. The American Heart Association indicates that more than five hundred thousand deaths are related to coronary artery disease and 170,000 deaths from stroke every year in this nation.

What is in red wine that is beneficial?

Ethanol is the fuel source. Polyphenolic composition of the wine is the useful compound or polyphenolic acid and alcohol. This prevents Atherosclerosis and improves the cardiovascular disease, lipid lowering effect, reduces the LDH ,the bad cholesterol improves / enhences the HDL, the good cholesterol produces vasodilatation or opening of the arteries possible delay the onset of Alzheimer disease is an antioxidant effect and may have protective effect on various cancer cell lines including human breast cancer, leukemia(blood cell cancers), and a few others polyphenol has also inhibit the platelet aggregation (stick together) which causes blood to clot, like Aspirin which has beneficial effect.

Alfredo C. Cordova, M.D., La Scienya M. Jackson M.D., David W. Berk-Schessel, Bauer E Sumpio M.D. PhD, from Yale University School of Medicine in New Haven, Connecticut reported in *The American College of Surgeons* March 2005.

I do not advise drinking alcoholic beverage. I just mention what is in the marketplace. You may drink adequate amount of red grape juice with crushed skin and seeds with the same beneficial positive effects of red wine. Pomegranate juice also has antioxidant affect, the power comes from the high content of polyphenols (anthocyanins, tannins, ellagic acid). It promotes heart health by reducing oxidation of LDL cholesterol and plaque build up, lowering blood pressure, inhibiting angiotension converting enzyme (ACE) and preventing the build up of plaque in the arteries. All factors that lead to the hardening of the (atherosclerosis).

Some of the side effects of alcohol dependence

Intoxication, cirrhosis of the liver (scarring of the liver) with or without ascites (fluid in the abdominal cavity), effects on the brain and many more side effects appear. Dr. James C. Garbutt from the University of Connecticut

School of Medicine and other authors state alcohol dependency is a major public health problem. It is worldwide the fourth leading cause of disability. Alcohol dependence is estimated in four per cent of the United States adult population and may contribute to more then one hundred thousand preventable deaths per year.
Addiction counseling, behavioral treatments and self-help, and Alcoholic Anonymous are available along with other organizations in the United States.

(*JAMA, The American Journal of the American Medical Association,* April 6, 2005). In France, the demand for liver transplantation is so high that surgeons use one donor liver for three recipients with cirrhosis of the liver related to excess alcohol intake. In the future the goal is to use one donor liver for more than three patients in the need of liver transplants.

Aspirin in Medicine

Hippocrates, the father of medicine, on the island of Cos, some two thousand four hundred years ago popularized white willow salicin, the precursor of Aspirin. He then wrote the first statement: Aphorism "Life is short, the art long opportunity fleeing, experiment treacherous and judgment difficult." Today life is longer but the art is longer still.

Physician Health study and various investigators centered at Harvard School of Public Health has now found that Aspirin significantly reduced the risk of myocardial infarction and stroke. (Even low dose Aspirin 30 to 81 mg a day is beneficial.) Richard I. Levin, M.D., *The New England Journal of Medicine,* March 31, 2005.

Chapter IX
Body and Soul

*I was created from minerality and became plants and from plants,
I recycled and became animal,
I died from animality and became man, then
Why fear disappearance through death?
Next time I shall die, Bring forth wings and feathers like angels
To what you cannot imagine I shall be that.*
                    Rumi, Persian Mystic

Summary

We human beings are as much spirit as flesh and bones. In ancient times, the Egyptian worshiped the "Sun God," Vedic ritual of India, the liberation of the individual soul by meditation and yoga in the East. And the ritual dances of the Dervishes (Sufi's) that were presented the key to open the door into Paradise with love and harmony toward mankind. The medicine wheel of the Native American Indians, the Chi energy in China, doctrine of the chakra energy circles in India, the journey of the spirit in the Northern part of Spain, and the houses of worship are all the pathways to the truth, peace and harmony in life. However, the "out of body experience" is a mysterious observation as I saw it.

Higher Self

According to Joseph Campbell and ancient Hindu philosophy, in India there is a system of seven psychological centers up the spine of the human body that is said that represents the energy points of concern, consciousness, and action. These are the seven energy centers or chakras: The seven energy centers or chakras are located down the spine from the pelvic area with sex organs to the top of the head. There are several other *chakras)*, like the palms of the hands, and the soles of the feet. These chakra centers radiate energies are representing different functions in the human body as well as animals.

The word chakra is Sanskrit, for circle, through these chakras the God cosmic forces or Prana (Sanskrit) enters the physical body to nourish various physical organs, the nervous system, the endocrine organs such as the pineal and pituitary glands, spleen, thymus, adrenals, liver, pancreas, gonads thyroid and parathyroid. When our chakras are healthy with the cosmic God forces they appear in the soul's body as swirling circles of light. Thus the lights of energy are like magnetic fields that can go up and down the spine and affects our systems directly. The Chinese identifies these energies as "Chi" and the Japanese call these energies "Ri" (Reiki).

The first center is called the <u>sex organs</u> and deals with pleasure and reproduction.

The second center is the rectum representing alimentation, the basic life-sustaining organ (large and small bowel).

The third center is the <u>navel or umbilical area</u> for ego, will power, mastering the animal instinct, competition, aggressiveness, and the master to conquer.

The fourth center is the <u>heart area</u> that is the center of giving, caring, sharing, and moving from animalistic stage to a human stage. The road to higher life, elevated thought, highways from the heart through love, mercy, and compassion with a higher energy of God's energy force. The physical body, the mind, and spiritual are what is said to be God's energies.

The fifth center is the <u>thyroid or larynx area</u> that works with communication, verbal ability, inspiration, truthfulness, creativity, voice, growth, and intelligence.

The sixth center is the <u>forehead area or center eye</u> to wisdom, intuition, awareness, pituitary gland (Mother gland, realization and self- knowledge.

The seventh center is the <u>top of the head</u> where we experience the higher planes, spirituality and knowledge of God, self-realization, and cosmic awareness.

> *To love another person is to see the face of God…*
> Victor Hugo

Our physical body is like a flower with beauty, perfume, and essences in which we can recognize our five senses and the spirit with holiness. Our body permeates energies with different frequencies, as well as the divine soul that is part of God's energy forces.

Where do I come from?

Excluding the human genetic and DNA engineering, Avicenna, Plato and others could not find a satisfactory explanation. St. Thomas Aquinas believed that God is absolutely simple and without composition. For centuries pilgrims have traveled thousands of miles over the mountains and seas looking in hopes of learning the secret of life.

Most people, however, believe there is a soul that is part of our spiritual body within us and leaves our body upon death. It is known that when someone dies, that the spiritual body leaves the earthly body and the earthly body becomes somewhat lighter. (This has been researched).

Spoken Name After Life

The Egyptians believed "to speak the name of the dead is to make them alive."

To these people this was of the utmost importance. If the body and image are destroyed, hopefully your name will remain intact. For example, the word <u>Ankhesamuns</u> has many spellings but the original name Ankhessehpaten means to live for Athens.

The Ancient Egyptian Concept of the Soul

To the ancient Egyptians, their being was composed of many different parts not only the physical forms but there were eight immortal or semi Divine parts that survived death and with the body making the ninth part of man. The eight are Khat(KHA)...Ka ... Ba..., Khaibit.... Akhu (Akh,Khu,Ikhu)....Sahu... AB(ib) and Ren.

Spirit

I hear beyond the range of sound, I see beyond the range of sight, new earths, and skies, and seas around, and in my noon the sun doth pale his lights.
    Henry David Toreau 1817-1862

What is soul?

According to the American dictionary, it is the spiritual, rational, and immortal part in man, the part of man that enables him to think, higher nature, and seat of life.

I personally believe that the spirit is a Godly state of purity, above and beyond the intellectual faculties of mankind.

Who maketh the clouds his chariot; who walketh upon the wings of the wind...
Psalms 104:3-4

Native American Spirituality

The Medicine Wheel. The medicine wheel represents the American Indian spirituality. This is the journey of man in life. The wheel shows the four cardinal directions (North, South, East and West) and the four sacred colors according to the Cherokee Indians. Fire and water are a symbol of purity. Similarly, in the Zarasthustian belief, ancient Persian religion, these two agents were part of their belief also. The Persian and Cherokee Indian believed that the number seven was sacred. There is a great Indian saying "Great Spirit, help me never to judge another until I have walked two weeks in his moccasins."

Ancient Persian Religion

The Zarathustrian religion uses the Holy Book of Avesta that presents the concept of one God for mankind with regards for Mother Nature (like...The American Indians). The doctrine of good thought, good words, and good deeds are rooted from that ancient faith and also their way of life.

Spiritual Path

- Walk the path of beauty of nature and acknowledge the radiance of creation.

- Open your heart, mind, and soul to yourself and others with love and compassion.
- Celebrate life on a daily basis. Let the spirit flow through you in a form of act of kindness. Recognize and accept that there is another dimension of life than what is obvious to you and beyond your five senses. Live and enjoy the present moment.
- The past is gone and the future is not here. Find the Divine energy in your daily life with love and share it with others.

Universal Energy

Life on Earth is more than one self and the three dimensional world. Energy exists within our being and everything around us. In Eastern philosophy, the spiritual life energy force of the Earth is called Prana. This Prana is entangled like the life force of the sun that is providing energy for all life. There is a famous pilgrimage that has taken people for centuries called the "Santiago de Compostela" Camino that is across part of Northern Spain. It is said by pilgrims, that the "Camino" is the road or a way that lies directly under the Milky Way and follows by the lines that reflect the energies from the star system above it. It is a state of consciousness where the journey of the soul is recognized.

Out of Body Experience

Why do I still return hauntingly to that night, during my

youthful surgical training and the frantic teamwork effort to save a fellow physician with a gunshot wound to the chest? No vital signs were present with a flat EKG, however, with proper resuscitation including open chest cardiac massage, the man survived.

The chilling yet enchanting realization was his depth of ability to talk about his "out of body experience" with extreme detail. He accounted for each team member, and their precise involvement and interaction, with his life saving procedure. He stated, "I was watching you from above." It is more than thirty five years later since that eventful night and I still do not know or understand this phenomenon.

During my many years of medical practice, I have met many adults and children with similar life stories. The "out of body experience" is both mysterious and enlightening as I am drawn back to revisit that angelic night with increasing thirst of love and interest. I do know we as human beings are as much Spirit as we are flesh and bones.

Dreams are part of it. Ruth Montgomery stated "Dreams are the language of the soul because you dream every night. It is important that we learn this language." The Eastern and Western philosophies have written many books on this spiritual subject. To mention a few: The Oxford history of Eastern and Western philosophy. Plato, Rumi, and Saint Thomas Aquinas had spiritual paths as well as the Hinduism and Buddhism.

Current societies turn to the television media and internet for the answers. There are live shows to satisfy the curiosity of the subject matter. Here are a few references: example:

A Journey of the Spirit by Shirley Maclaine,
Embraced by the Light by Betty J. Eadie,
Forward by Melvin Morse, MD,
Talking to Heaven by James Van Praagh,
Crossing Over by John Edwards,
Body, Mind and Soul by Deepak Chopra, MD.

As I mentioned earlier, the physical body, the mind, and spiritual body are all part of the same universal energy, God force energy, call it nature or call it anything that your heart desires. I can see the face of God in nature and everything around me. "Love is a cycle situation; first he loved man so that man could love him, man in his own image." (The Bible)

Chapter x

Art of Converting the Inner Pain to Happiness

Ah, my beloved, fill up the cup that is clear today of past regrets and future fears tomorrow? Why tomorrow I may be myself with yesterday's seven thousand years.
Omar Kayyam
Persian Poet, Physicist, and Astronomer

A positive inner-light can overcome our anger in day to day life experiences. Tolerance and patience have great benefits. For instance, mediation can create a calm atmosphere to concentrate with a clear mind in order to turn a negative thought to a positive one; the human body has all the hormones, neuro-peptides and other amino acids to regulate and sustain a normal healthy life.

The gift of giving and giving a helping hand make people feel good about themselves. Even at a time of disaster such as "Superman" after his riding accident he will be remembered as Superman. However, our expectations should be realistic. Good things do not happen without training, educational experience and action. Finally live for a higher purpose; remember that your soul is part of you.

Finding the Root of Pain or What Makes us "Happy"

External pain, like daily pain of Rheumatoid Arthritis with morning stiffness, and swelling, and disfigurement of joints, we can see and manage accordingly. But internal pain and perception of that pain which we can not explain physically is a different matter.

From birth to death we need love, caring, and sharing. Researchers at Washington University studied the effect of soft music played in the neonatal intensive care that gives premature infants a better chance of life with regular heart rates, respiration, oxygen saturation, and sucking responses.

Even better, a mother's gentle humming and massaging improves the oxygen saturation and weight gains. The gentle touch and soft voice and music can play a role in the brain waves and development. Harsh music has the opposite effect. This principle is also true in growth and development, we are here to learn from our children as well as teach them. Adult music therapy can help patients relax and cope better with stress and pain of serious illness like cancer. (JAMA, February 2000)

A child is a fragile human being. Parent's participation in

the care of children is beneficial to the family unit, for growth and development. The joy of raising an intact family is a giant step which every father and mother should experience it with pleasure. This is a journey towards happiness and a treasure which lasts towards maturity and beyond.

A study by Barlow et al 1996, showed that fear and anxiety affects the entire family in a negative way. Other researchers from Texas University reported (Journal of Pain, January 2000) that fear has a different affect on human pain thresholds at different times. One thing is clear that happiness brings happiness and love brings love most of the time. Fear is a normal mechanism of the body to take action response.(fight/flight)

Acute trauma or shock of various etiologies are associated with an increase of circulating levels of endogenous opioid substances, the most common of which appears to b e Beta-endorphine(parallel to morphine.) Chronic fear and anxiety can create emotional distress and depression which we get upset, loose our appetite, or overeat could be signs of depression.

The terminology of "gut feeling" also has a proper meaning. At lest five types of mucosal receptors are present in the gastrointestinal tract. These include mechanical, chemical, osmotic, thermal, and painful sensations. A light touch in the throat from food containing acid or alkali, or hot or cold liquid entering our stomach or bowel can affect us one way or another.

However, complex inner hormones and peptides with different pathways in the human body from the hypothalamus gland in the brain to each system in the body with each specialized cell function are fascinating art of nature. (Brain gut peptides) The hypothalamus is in charge of the four "F." fever, fleeing, fighting, feeding and mating. This is a gland located above the pituitary gland or the mother gland.

Research suggests that imbalance in body function emotional distress and reactivity can cause diseases in the human. Like ulcerative colitis, Crohn's disease (infection plus psychological factors) and many other diseases.

Sigmund Freud, father of Psychoanalysis Therapy, said many mental processes are entirely unobservable. When trauma or disaster happens people may choose two directions. One way is a positive way with motivation towards something good for themselves and humanity or under pressure they accept defeat, depression and a downhill course.

Stress, Coping, and Health

Good thought, good words, good deeds
Zoroaster
Sixth Century BC Persian Prophet

Gift of Life

A seven year old boy, Micheal, died in 1999 as a result of a gunshot wound at the base of the skull. The senseless act of violence shocked the parents of the boy. His organs were donated to seven children in need of organ transplants. This gift of life affected so many people in a positive way that a number of clinics have been built for Micheal. What a lovely memory.

"I do not have time to die"

A sixty- five year old grandmother was diagnosed to have inflammatory carcinoma of the breast, which is a serious type to have with a short duration of survival. During her follow-up she told our radio-therapist that "I don't have time to die, since I have to take care of my grandchild while my daughter is attending college." This wonderful women, kept her promise with determination to the last moment, over three years after her diagnosis.

We may not always realize that everything we do affects not only our lives but touches others too. For a little bit of thoughtfulness that shows someone you care creates a ray of sunshine for both of you to share. Every time you offer someone a helping hand, every time you show a friend you care and understand, every time you have a kind and gentle word to give you help someone find beauty in this precious life we live. Happiness brings happiness and a loving way brings love and giving is the treasure of contentment.

Do we need each other?

Stories have been told in Greek mythology that the inhabitants of the earth were round, self sufficient, sexless and selfish creatures with four hands and four legs. They were arrogant and repeatedly attacked the God. (Zeus) God split them apart; now two incomplete creatures. They always acted like they were missing something, (like Adam and Eve) later merging developed between them with passion, love, and sometimes with meanness and selfishness. According to Rumi and later the Dalai Lama; "Within all beings there is a seed of perfection." Find it accordingly. We as human beings really need each other one way or another.

Relationships

> *Only the beauties' love my heart will accept*
> *For anything but love, I have no concept.*
> Hafez
> Thirteen Century Persian Poet

"Loneliness is hazardous to your health." People who come together for functional or even minimal reasons discover that they like one another. In churches, temples, mosques, schools and clubs - how do people come to like one another?

Researchers suggest that "liking" provides a useful bridge to social interaction. Women seem to share certain similarities. Conventional wisdom says, people of the same nature come together whether in shopping malls, fashion shows and etc.

You may ask what this discussion has to do with anything about personal happiness. At a personal level, sharing and self-disclosure between two people makes the beginning of a relationship that sets them apart of each other. All of us have/had this experience; it is quite wonderful one and yet to discover that there is another person who thinks, feels, and experiences the world "just as I do."

People in this category are generally motivated to continue their relationship to discover if their other values and commitments permit a depth to the relationship. Connection or association through blood or marriage is some thing we can cherish.

A friend with moral values (integrity) is one you want to keep. Friendships that are based on wealth, power, or position; in these cases your friendship continues as long as your power, wealth, or position is sustained otherwise the friendship disappears.

In love and marriage, ninety percent of adults in North America marry at least once. Mark Twain quotes "No man or woman really know what perfect love is until they have been married a quarter of a century. In a relationship, compassion is an essential part of it as well as healthy communication is a basic foundation of a good marriage.

Why loneliness is hazardous to your health?

This is because antisocial behavior may lead to mood changes and depression. Some people may substitute their boredom with excess food or alcohol intake or other crutches. Archeological evidence suggests that humans were drinking one form of alcohol or another before 6000 BC. In moderation drinking seems to make most people feel relaxed, sociable and easy going. In excess, however alcohol leads to dullness of sensation, degrade sensory motor performance, impaired thought process, sleep disturbance, and even death.

A Persian poet explained this phenomenon very well that is titled "Lost Magic" by Feraydoon Moshiri, translated and revised by me which go as this;

Lost Magic
Fill up your cup

Fill up the cup, take me to the places where you have brought me before.
These jugs which are emptied one after another
Are like fire, which are melting my desire.
I have had a long relationship with wine,
Hiding it secrets and magic.
We have traveled together many times to the
Places that you have never dreamed before.
Visited cities in foreign lands,

Passing through many narrow streets
Observing exotic gardens, swimming in creeks.
We have seen the stars at the edge of the universe come and go
Even experienced life and death
Oh! My friends, what is happening to me?
The magic secret does not work any more
Hi eagle of love,
Rise from the cloud at the mountain-top
To the fields of my dreams
Carry me to the places
Which wine cannot do it any longer?
Looks like in the garden of life
With all the desires, wishes, and expectations,
I am still laughing and shouting
I am thirsty…. I am thirsty
Fill up the cup.

Rich in Heart and Mind

It is better to wear out than rust out.
Bishop Richard Cumberland
1637-1718

In order to be happy we do not need more money. We do not need greater success or fame or the perfect mate right now. At this very moment we have a "mind" which has all the basic equipment we need to achieve complete happiness. According to the Dalai Lama when we refer to "mind" or consciousness there are many different varieties; just like external conditions or objects are sometime useful, sometimes very harmful and some neutral.

So when dealing with external matter usually we try to identify which of these different substances or chemicals are helpful, so we can take care to cultivate, increase and use them. Those substances that are harmful, we need to discard them. Similarly, when we talk about the mind, there are thousands of different "thoughts" or different "mind" among them. Some are very helpful, those we should take and nourish, while some are harmful and negative and those we should try to reduce or eliminate. The first step in seeking happiness is self-motivation and learning.

Achieving Happiness

Abraham Maslow (1970) saw human motivation as a "step ladder needs" with the most basic being physiological need and the highest being self. Actualization (our spirit and our dreams) are only after the basic needs are satisfied then we can work on achieving higher needs (spiritual life.)

Step I
    Physiological needs   hunger, thirst, sex, etc.

Step II
    Safety needs   shelter, security

Step III
    Need to belong   affiliate, love, and to be accepted

Step IV
    Need for self esteem   approval and respect

Step V
    Self Actualization   to be all that you can be

Most human beings have a strong drive to educate themselves to have a master skill and to achieve long term goals with balance in life. (Family, work, and spirituality) No one said this life is easy.

In the twenty- first century we have to work harder to learn the rules of the game. We have to change our state of mind from negative to positive by overcoming negative behaviors, which requires many steps. Our first step involves learning through *education*. Education and learning are important because they help one develop *conviction* for the need to change and increase one's *commitment*. The next step, one transforms determination into *action*. People often want to make positive changes in their lives by engaging in healthier behaviors, but motivation is not there or they are lazy to do something about it.

Dalai Lama suggests "Patience" for long term problems. "As long as space endures, as long as sentient being remains may I too live to dispel the miseries of the world." This verse may have merit as in the case of the fall of the communist totalitarian regimes and may not work for solving problems in our daily life.

In some situations we need to take the proper action with a realistic expectation, otherwise we loose hope. Today we need to upgrade our knowledge and learn new skill, in the fast pace, growing world of technology. I find that our daily life is challenging. I am expressing my inner feelings with my children through letters. One special letter I will share with you is called:

Path of Life

Today December 02, 1997, while walking along the shore of the majestic Pacific Ocean, following two days of rain and storms, I noted major changes: The beautiful sun was shining and the blue water with high waves were advancing and advancing toward the shore, washing the sand and pushing everything in it way including the rocks. The usual smooth path on the sand no longer existed, creating a challenge for surfers as well as the walkers on the beach.

I enjoyed walking at the edge, with the unpredictable waves against my body while trying to climb on rocks. I compared this event to our daily lives with its unexpected hardships and variable challenges to follow. For someone who looks for fairness in life, these changes can cause stress and fright which can be a way of life. For the one who enjoys the challenges this can be a way to achievement and success.

My friend, which way is your way?
M. Mir, MD
Depth of Perception

Chapter XI
Seven Steps To Heaven

All men by nature desire to learn
Aristotle

In search of the truth, we have to look beyond the scientific or physical reality. As Rumi stated: "I was a hidden treasure and I wanted to be known, so I created man that be known one must be educated by one's heart to things which cannot be known otherwise."

Light

Ancient Parsies (Farsis), believed that the first thing God created was the light. Rumi stated, "Let the light shine in your heart and soul." Note from the cosmos suggests that the energy which separated from the big energy (big bang) someday will go back to the maker, as the universe expands and reunites again.

Isaac Newton (1612-1727), an English physicist who profoundly influenced the eighteenth century through thought. He formulated the laws of gravity, invented the reflecting telescope, and discovered how a prism resolves white light into many spectrums of color.

The light gives us life and the star we live by is the sun. No other object in the universe is as important as the sun. The sun is the central fire upon which any life there may be elsewhere in the solar systems exists. Less than a century ago, no one knew how the solar furnace really worked. Now with the principles of nuclear fusion understood, man not only knows what processes is going on in the sun, but he can even duplicate them. After the birth of light comes the birth of life. There has been life before us and there will be life after us.

Life

What is life? Could it be a biological existence of all creatures, including human beings? For man, the physical, mental, and spiritual experiences is that of life? How can one cell start and how does the cell know what to do is the question.

In biology, perhaps even more than other sciences, much is still theory and not necessarily fact. The brain of every cell has an information center called "DNA," the basic material of the gene. It is a fact that every one of our cells contains all the genes that we may inherit from our parents. This means that each cell has a complete set of blueprints for creating every structure in our body and performing every bodily function. What is even more fascinating, each cell is unique doing its own task without confusion. What initiates this selection process? Perhaps it may be a chemical, hormonal, or an enzyme compound within the cell that can turn off most of the genes and yet allow only a few active ones to tell the cell what to do. Maybe some particular genes are activated at a particular time when they are needed. When God created Adam and Eve, he planted the seed of knowledge (DNA) in every cell in their bodies with love.

Dervishes looked at life with ease, flying like a bird, a freedom from the material world, outpouring of feelings and thoughts; which describes the natural state of man so unfamiliar to the ordinary life while accepting responsibilities in life.

Rumi, 1207-1273, a Sufi, a Persian poet, philosopher, teacher, and a family man was a good example of a complete spiritual being. He lived all of his life with the thought of God (Zikr) and practiced his gift of love towards humanity. According to his teachings, love is spiritual growth and life without love is not living.

Life on Earth is more than just self and our three-dimensional world. Energy exists within us and everything has energy around us.

Love

Love is defined as "the will to extend one's self for the purpose of nurturing one's own or another spiritual growth." Symbols of love have been expressed in the past in forms of art, music, medicine, religion and so on. Among the earliest know pieces of art in the world are the so-called "Venus" of the Stone Age in Europe.

One of the "Venus" of the Willendorf was discovered in Austria and is believed to be over twenty thousand years old. There was also a discovery in Egypt of a God of fertility representing the masculine male. Michelangelo in Italy (1501) made a colossal marble figure of youthful David. His work was largely inspired by what he knew of Greek and Roman status.

The paradox that we, human beings chose the word "love" raises the question of whether this is true love or there is not love at all? With love comes responsibility, according to Buddha; the true love is, "A gift of finding valuable or agreeable things not sought for, a true love needs preparation and seeking for it."

We have in America more than twenty different definitions that have been recorded for the name of "love" from a deep feeling of affection and solicitude toward a person, amour or amorous, to love in mythology and love in theory. Deep love toward a child, parent, friends, and family are easy to understand but the love of objects and animals are a different matter.

Love is not an emergency. When sex is in a state of emergency the "amour" is an illusion and the act of love making strikes like the thunder by passing the control center of the body's processes. The brain and the body usually "talk" to each other through the hypothalamus-pituitary connection. The hypothalamus is just a tiny cluster of cells in the brain. This gland monitors the information about the state of the body. It is also a main coordinator of activities in the nervous system, thus it can be considered an intermediary between the brain and the body.

The mechanisms by which they talk to each other are known today. Messages that travel to and from the brain travel through the hypothalamus and the pituitary pathways. Let us consider those organs that are related to the senses that are aware of the phenomenon, such as a beautiful sunrise, a painful bee sting, smelling the perfume of a rose and call it the "conscious mind" with awareness. The conscious mind follows a well-regulated physiological adjustment and normal feedback. But some communication between the brain and the body may function independently like "emergency love" which can manifest itself into a state of confusion, regulated by other glands or hormones in the body like sex hormones, resulting in a pleasurable experience that is short lived. The "unconscious mind" may communicate to us when we are awake or when we are asleep. Discipline can be practiced when we are awake.

From ancient times to the modern day a 300 gram, pear shaped pump the so called heart has been blamed for the secret of all actions related to human sexuality.
Hafez, a Persian poet wrote his inspiration.

> *The love of my darling sets my heart on fire*
> *A fire that burns with pleasure, my entire desire*
> *Come close, my love, and tell me no tale,*
> *Your tender lips are precious rubies to share.*
> *My body may not have you always to embrace*
> *My heart is always at your treasury of grace.*

The heart is one of the energy centers of the body. It is the seat of unconditional love. Here the higher spiritual elements of nutrition, trust, giving, receiving, and nurturing are felt. Here is the desire to help humanity. Like the brain, the hypothalamus, pituitary and pineal gland, it has high-energy waves.

Learn

Learning means growing up to be responsible. Once we truly know that life is difficult, once we truly understand and accept it, then life is no longer difficult. Life is a series of problems. Learning to solve the problems can be although challenging at times and yet it may be enjoyable as well.

Practically all children have a tendency to deny their responsibility as an immature reflex related to conflicts. This is portrayed by blaming siblings, friends, and others for their own shortcomings. For some, this may carry over as a habit into their adult life.

Learning with love is a very important early in life. It is usually one step at a time experience, a lengthy and successful maturation that we can gain the capacity to see the world and our place in it realistically. Thus, learn to assess our responsibilities form ourselves, our family, and society.

There is much that parents can do to assist their children in this important maturation. Teaching and learning needs time, willingness, love and most of all effort. I will again reiterate I cannot forget the few hours that we spent together with my family and friends in preparation of the "ash soup". We spoke of our family history, told colorful stories, spoke about the dervishes, read poetry by Saadi and Hafez and prayed. There was a lot of hugging, kissing, laughing, learning of traditions and respect for each other. The family had unity, love, and caring which builds up the immune mechanism and moral love for self and love for others.

The Universe is our home says the Lord,
He who gives the sun to light the day,
Moon and stars to light the night,
Who stirs up the sea til its wave roar,
Whose name is the Lord of host.
Holy Bible

Land

As early as 4000 BC in the valley of the Tigris and the Euphrates rivers, the plains of Babylonia, and the Sumarian civilization had recognized floods as the source of wealth as well as disaster.

Many religious stories started from Ur and Babylon, an example The Prophet Abraham (2000BC) father of Isaac and Ishmael, descendants, and including Joseph, historically were born in "Ur," a most important portion of Sumarian towns and indeed the nucleus of its civilization were the temple enclosures.

Here were places surrounded and protected by massive wall built of sun baked brick. Around the temple were built houses. The chief ruler of the town was also the priest. To this sanctuary, under the shadow of the towering temple, the peasants brought their offerings, which were usually a goat, a jar of water containing green palm branches intended to symbolize the vegetables, life of the land, and which God maintained with the annual rainfall and swollen rivers.

The worshiper's jar with green palm branches later on became "The Tree of Life," a symbol often depicted on city monuments. These gifts the worshiper's laid before the God of Earth and Heaven. The peasants prayed for plentiful water and generous harvests. They also prayed for deliverance from destructive floods that the God had once sent to overwhelm the land. The peasant farmers had told their children of these catastrophes while passing their traditions.

These stories of the flood passed over to the Hebrews and later into the Holy Bible. How did religion begin? Due to human needs? Fear or Faith? The Babylonian religion itself was an adaptation of the earlier Sumerian creeds. Babylon was famous for hanging flowering baskets and great walls, yet a great civilization over 4000 years, BC.

Legacy is to create a nurturing
A place of faith with love, truth, and happiness

Legacy

What we leave behind for our children, family, and society is dependent on the health of our parents and their relationships. In reality, genetic makeup is a starting point, and the rest are choices we make in life with responsibility. In the physical world we have to remove the mask and face reality:

Physical reality: our bodies and the world around us
Mental reality: our thoughts
Spiritual reality: a journey toward ultimate truth, a higher consciousness or God

How can we face reality? We are growing and changing yet we have to find a direction. The problem of map making is not to start from scratch but we must strive to be accurate. In all changing and challenging atmospheres, galaxies come and go and also cultures come and go. When there is abundant technology even more dramatically the world will be constantly changing.

If we want to be a good teacher we must be good listeners and gain knowledge with it. When we were children we were dependent and powerless. As adults we may become powerful and yet if old age or one serious illness happens then again it makes us powerless and dependent again, as I have experienced it.

A recent study by the World Health Organization (WHO) showed that people seek health care not for pain only but for diagnosis and symptom relief. Pain interferes with daily activities, family relationships, causes worry and emotional distress, and undermines the confidence in one's health. Another study from Canada suggested that a patient used spirituality and their own intuition in their treatment was a more effective way, than scientific options alone. I personally believe the most crucial aspect of legacy is a loving family relationship regardless of all the other external factors.

Behind any magnificent structure there is a designer, call him Lord, call him God, Allah, Yahweh, a divine being and the great light.

Lord

When you have a well-regulated, well-organized system in every cell of every living creature on earth and elsewhere, regulated seasons, planets and the magnificent universe, it is hard to believe all this happened as a random occurrence.

Prehistoric man and cultures existed over 500,000 years ago! What type of culture were they? We just don't know. Religion is a part of the earlier attempts of the human mind to achieve a sense of security in the real world.

> *O ancient cousin. What love had you? What words to speak? What worship, Cousin?*
> (Quote from Stone Age Europe)

In the beginning, God of heaven and earth... God said "Let there be light and there was light. God saw the light was good and he separated the light from darkness. God called the light "day" and the darkness he called "night." Seven days. Genesis. The Holy Bible.

When God created man and he planted the seed of knowledge of DNA in every cell of Adam and Eve, God created man in his own image. He created male and female. He created them with the seed of knowledge he gave them human fulfillment of higher potentialities of life, mind, and Spirit. Spirit is energy within us and around us. We have one creator with dynamic energy of one God, one ancestor, and one root to all mankind.

So if there is one God, one origin, one universe, then why do we have so many differences? We all have religion… according to the Holy Books, then the super power is of one source. And make no mistake I am not agnostic, as I believe in the existence of God. The analogy "Good thought, good word, good deeds" is the same logic which has been recorded by the ancient Persian faith Zoroastrian (Ahura Mazda) over thousands of years ago.

Lessons to Remember

Our spirit does not go to the higher level unless we earn it. When you exclude the physical body, the spirit or soul is free to be.

Distance from the earth to heaven is human perception. When God takes over, the time and space do not mean anything,

In search of truth, the human mind needs to be open about everything in order to understand and feel the true meanings of love, life, relationship, religion and so on.

Rumi stated "In everyone and everything there is something good, find it as you would search in the ocean for a shiny pearl in the heart of a shell"

Regardless of what religion we have, there is one source and one God only. Even for the Native American Indian and other cultures their belief was in God.

In 1855, when President Franklin Pierce stated that he would buy the land of the Chief Seattle's tribe from them, the Chief wrote a long and philosophical letter stating "How can you buy or sell the sky? The land? This idea is strange to us." At the closing of the letter Chief Seattle wrote, "One thing we know, our God is also your God."

So if there is one origin, one God, and one universe, then why do we have so many conflicts? Maybe we should start all over again?

Chapter XII

Sufism

If one doesn't yet understand how to serve the people, how can one understand serving spirit and God.
Confucious 551-497 BC

*When you are everywhere, you are nowhere,
When you are somewhere, you are everywhere.*
Rumi

The word "Sufi" is derived from Suf (wool), a cloth used by the ancient holy men, some to Safi (pure) and the Persian word Darwish (literally means the metal door knocker) is accepted in Turkish and Arabic. The Greek word "sophos" means awareness in life, on a higher plane than on which we live. (Rumi)

History of Sufism

The history of Sufis has a complicated course. A high mystical faith rooted from the old history of Mohamadism, however, this faith is not limited to Islam.

The Prophets are perfect men by whom the hidden nature of God is revealed, they are essentially one with God and with each other (Koran).

According to Mohamad's statement "The first thing that God created was the light." Rumi said, "Follow the light in your heart and soul." Jellal U Ddin "Rumi", the writer of a famous book, <u>The Mesnevi</u>, with multiple chapters in Farsi each have four hundred to six hundred pages. It contains strange and rare stories, lovely sayings, profound indications, a way for the holy, and a garden for the pious believers. It holds the roots of the faith and gifts of mysteries of the spiritual knowledge.

The Doctrine of the Sufism is of the human divinity and unity with the maker.

Co-existing they hold that God is imminent in spirit and in substance in the universe. That only real love in the Universe is that love, which relates us with perfection - all other love being a dream to vanish at dawn.

Eternity has neither beginning nor end. Its aim is bliss. (I personally think the beginning is the end and end is the beginning.) Sufism is love for human beings and it brings the humanity the culture of mankind. True love, the one that Mevlana "Rumi" offers is the love with knowledge. "God speaks to everyone", a Hadith states "I was a hidden treasure and I wanted to be known, first there is knowledge not the knowledge of the head, but the knowledge in the heart, one must be educated by love and compassion to the things which can not be understood otherwise intellectually. Love is a cyclic situation and God loves all the creatures. First he loved man in his own image, "I created man in my own image and into him, I insufflated of my own Spirit."

The First Famous Sufi Woman

Neither Arab nor Mongol invasion could totally destroy the Persian culture. "Strangely," the first famous Sufi was a woman, "Rabia", who died a century and a half, after the beginning of the Moslem era. Delightful story after story is told of ecstatic passion for the adored, yet spiritual indeed. She was highly respected. She declared that she reached God by losing in him all ease that she had found. Crying aloud that she yearned to see God, she drew nearer, nearer by any means. She was answered by the voice in her heart. "O Rabia, have you not heard that when Moses desired to see God, only a mote of the Divine majesty fell on a mountain and scattered it in fragments, be content therefore with my name."

When asked by what means she had attained this intimate knowledge, she replied "Others know by certain ways and means, but I without ways and without means." And she continues speaking. Rabia was sincere in her prayers and felt the shining light of the Lord in her heart and in her soul. This spirit was to blossom with the fruits of the labor in her poetry, and the music of Sadi, Jellal U Ddin Rumi, Hafez and others also.

Sufi orders and initiation started during the time of the Prophet Muhammad and continued with the growth of many circles of teachings in Persia, Turkey, India, Iraq, North and East Africa, Spain, Egypt and eventually traveled to the West.

Sufism became a philosophy of life for many people. An uneasy yet necessary relationship between the King and the Dervishes (Sufi) was beautifully illustrated by the Persian Poet Sadi, in the "Golestan Sadi," A Rose Garden of 1248, "A kind Dervish was wearing the crown of a King"

Sufi Orders of Rituals and Initiations

Dervishes usually follow the rules that have been codified by the founding figures. They do not take the vow of celibacy as done by the Christian Monks and Nuns, nor do they have a central authority such as a Pope. The Authority of Sufi teachers are based on the teachings of Prophets, the Messengers of God, and prayer is part of their daily life.

At the time of initiation, some men shave their heads without shaving their face, purification of the body is done by water (like a baptismal ceremony), and purification of the soul is done by prayer (Zikr) after repeating the names of previous saints, Imam, example Ali, son in law of Muhammad), the brotherhood tree of meditations, and the mystical experience of the ritual dancing to the sound of the flute, highlights the Sufim ritual. The ceremony finished with the serving of tea, sweets and fruits. The ritual may vary in different parts of the world, especially in India, the Orient, Turkey, and in the West.

Colorful Cloaks

According to the Biblical scriptures, a colorful wrap was the symbol of the "shirt" that Gabriel provided to the Prophet Abraham with when Nimrod threw him naked into the fire. Some Sufis refer to the "shirt" given to the Prophet by Gabriel was worn by him during his Ascension. This biblical story became tradition by the Masters to their followers over the generations and suggests "The sign of the possibility of the presence of God, also in the outfits of the Disciples. See Divine mercy and Grace." Dervishes in Persia usually wear a loose colorful or simple garment or robe.

Rules to Follow

Abu said the Sufi Master listed ten rules to applying to communal life:
- **Purity**
  Constant prayer to keep god in mind and heart at all times.
  Meditations...visions...how to listen to one's higher self
- **Hospitality**
- **Giving**
  Teachings... ethics... etc
- **Morality**
  Traveling... Communicating with self and other
  How to behave during performances of music and poetry
  How to avoid intoxication

Later the rules became more elaborated, including the mediation, respect for Mother Nature and the rules of the Sufi garments. Other rules included how to respect the teachers, how to respond to the offerings of food when fasting, and how to deal with pride in one's literary accomplishments. Disciples of Sufi are warned to refrain from the company of mad galanders (drunken hippies), of wine and disrespectful Sufi's. Rumi stated "think on the mercies of God and the love of God."

Barrow (Barrow-Isaac 1630-1677) an English theologian, scholar and mathematician sums up some of the philosophy of the Sufi's as though he had been one of them, here or possibly East or West, certainly they have met.

"Love is the sweetest and most delightful of all passions. When the conduct of wisdom, is directed in a rational way toward a worthy cause, yet it cannot do otherwise than fill the heart with ravishing delight. Such in respect, superlatively such, is God, our soul from its original instinct verges toward him and can have no rest until it can be fixed on him. He alone can satisfy the vast capacity of our mind and fulfill our boundless desires. He cherishes and encourages our love by sweet embrace. We cannot fix our eyes upon the Infinite beauty we cannot taste infinite sweetness without forever rejoicing in the first daughter of love to God, charity toward man." During my early life I felt and embraced by the Divine fruits of Sufism, since my great uncle was a highly educated Sufi Master, and lived dedicated this philosophy throughout his entire lifetime.

Sufi Codes... Meanings

1. Sleep means deep meditation
2. Perfume is the indication of the divine presence
3. Kisses and embrace are the mystic union of Divine love
4. God (Allah) the saver, the creator
5. Wine is the spirit
6. Tavern is the house of worship
7. Intoxication is not by wine but the love of God
8. State of oneness is the union with God

Stories of life are written in Mesnevi, as life itself
Music... the sound of the flute is a heavenly message
That men suddenly dazzled lose themselves in ecstasy before a mortal shrine whose light is but a shade of the Divine, not 'til thy secret beauty through the cheek... The power of Sufi poetry is born not only by the students of the faith, but also by the deep and emotional debates that have surrounded its interpretations by the Western teachers. If you seek to soar to the heaven and make friends with all men (Mecca of the heart) when the seed of love is planted in the heart of the believers only God know where it will bare fruit. The whirling dance (Sema) is like a spiritual field of energy where one can plant seeds of faith. (Sema is the traditional dance of the whirling Dervishes in Iran, Turkey and elsewhere).

"I am he whom I love and he whom I love is I, we are two spirits dwelling in one body of you see me you see him, and seeing him you see us both. Strangely, it is in Jesus that he sees the light of God. Hallaj, a Sufi master said "I am being killed and crucified and my hands and feet are cut off but I do not recant." Thus it is told by a friend who observed that "when Husayn Ibn Mansur al Hallaj was brought forward to be crucified and saw the cross and the nails, he laughed so greatly that the tears stood in his eyes." He knelt, on a prayer carpet, of another friend and received the prayer (Fatehe) and a verse from the Koran. He also prayed for the servants whom had gathered to slay him, and asked the Lord to have mercy upon them. His friend on his side was speechless. "Kill me" he said "that you may be rewarded and I have rest, for so you will a fighter for the faith and I a martyr."

Mevlana Jalal u Ddin Rumi

Rumi was born in the city of Balkh, the mother of all cities. His father, Baha u din, was a famous spiritual leader and his mother came from a royal family in Khwarazm. His father predicted the Mongol's destruction of Balkh. He assembled a large caravan of friends, students, family and left Balkh across the vast land of Persia towards Mecca. As predicted, Gengis Khan's army burned the cultural centers of Balkh, slaughtered people in other cities and burned books including over 15,000 Korans.

Sixteen years later, Baha'u din and his family settled in Konya (present time Turkey). Young Jalaj u ddin Rumi was schooled while traveling and became master in reading the Koran. In Nishabur, Northeast Persia, a Sufi master and chemist named Farid al din Attar, gave the young Jalal u ddin his blessing and a copy of his book of mysteries. Attar told Baha u din, "A day will come when this child will kindle the fire of Divine enthusiasm throughout the world." Attar published one hundred fourteen books including memoirs of the saints and conferences of the birds.

Jalal u ddin Rumi married a young woman named Gevher Khatun. Rumi's father became the founder of a school (medresah, a learning center) in Karaman. In a few years Jalal u ddin became a full scholar and raised a garden of flowers and fruit on the side.

Sultan Alaeddin invited Baha u din Rumi and his son to the University as a professor and advisor. Jalal u ddin Rumi, a noble scholar of theology, became successor to his father and taught many students from different countries.

Rumi slept very little, accumulated many books and held a position at Konya University (Turkey). He stated he was reaching a level of "walking on water." The universe is an ocean of vibrations and each movement is a wave of the great devotees praying to be liberated so that they may be able to swim in this ocean. The greatest of the devotees are able to rise above the wave of this vast ocean of life where so many are drowned. To be in the world but not of it is to "walk on water." The constant repetition of "Zikr" was carrying Rumi above the concepts of the Earth. Rumi had a vision and the ability to trace a man's past and read his future by experiencing his presence. He had the power of spiritual healing.

"The nation of love differs from all other lovers, bare alliance to no nation or sect" stated Rumi.

Chapter XIII

History of People with Vision

Chinese philosopher committed to Humanizing the existence of people, urged:
Not to do to others what you would not want them to do to you.
Confucius (551-479 BC)

Since the beginning of time there have been millions of people in the world with extraordinary knowledge and vision, who have devoted their time and effort toward the progress of mankind. I am mentioning only a few people's names that have practiced the doctrine of: "Good thoughts, good words and good deeds." Some were for the well being of humanity and a few others with their discoveries that have changed the course of history. Keep in mind that we have one life to live, one Earth to respect, and only one God to worship.

Mother Teresa (1910-1996)

She was born August 27, 1910 in Sknopje, Yugoslavia-Macedonia, a woman who hungered for love. She was named "the spirit of India" for helping the poorest people in Calcutta, India (over 50,000 alone) and expanded her mission all over the world to help orphans afflicted with handicaps and leprosy as well as anyone else who needed her help. Mother Teresa collected over sixty five billion dollars. Most of it was coming from governments and wealthy individuals. She devoted herself for the helpless people worldwide. On a 1981 visit to New York she received a ceremonial key to New York City after winning the Nobel Prize in 1979 for her good deeds. Mother Teresa and her co-workers as well as Mahatma Gandhi shared a prayer of Saint Francis of Assisi:

> *Lord, make me a channel of peace*
> *That where there is despair I may bring hope*
> *That where there is a shadow I may bring light*
> *That where there is sadness, I may bring joy.*

September 11, 2001 disaster was the day of rebirth of many Mother Teresa and Gandhi. During my December visit to ground zero, I noted that despite the psychological and economical disaster, the people of New York City were coping with the unexpected…yet hope, faith, and "spiro" was alive.

The Former Princess of Wales, Sarah Ferguson, had an office at the 101st floor of the World Trade Center. She reported that a hand made doll on the window-sill of that 101st floor was found in the ruble and had survived the fall and fire intact.

Similar dolls are now used to raise money to help children in Afghanistan as a symbol; of survival of love and faith.

Gandhi-known as Mahatma (1869-1948)

He was a nationalist, a spiritual leader of India, who developed the practice of non-violence, and who forced Great Britain to grant India independence in 1947. On March 12, 1930, during a two hundred mile peace march from Sabarmati to Dandi, India, Gandhi delivered his first message to the Indian people as he passed from village to village. He said; "To keep clean, abandon child marriages, avoid drug and alcohol use and live purely." Gandhi stated "act but seek not the fruit of your action, for your action flows out to the person whom you are in love with. It is a bit like being in love. Love will just flow to the person you are in love with." When speaking of the Great Mahatma, physicist Albert Einstein once stated "Generations to come. It may be, will scarcely believe that such a one as this ever in the flesh and blood walked upon this earth." A Hindu fanatic assassinated Gandhi in 1948.

Albert Einstein (1879-1955)

Albert Einstein was a German born American theoretical physicist whose general and special theories of relativity revolutionized modern thought on the nature of space and atomic energy. He was presented a Nobel Prize in 1921 for his explanation of the photo-electronic effect. His statement was "Nothing happens until something moves."

Madam Marie Curie - born Manja Skiodowska (1867-1934)

She was a Polish born French trained chemist. Madam Curie shared a 1903 Nobel Prize with her husband Pierre Curie (1859-1906) and Henri Becqueri for the fundamental research on radioactivity. Again in 1911, she won a second Nobel Prize for her discovery and study of radium and plutonium. Madam Curie's achievement also demonstrated to the world that women could perform intellectually and brilliantly while fulfilling a warm, loving marriage, and bringing up two children.

Joseph Lister (1827-1912)

He was a British surgeon who demonstrated that carbolic acid was an effective antiseptic agent in 1865. Lister had a prestigious position in Glasgow, Scotland, a place known for the intellectual individuals who were working on germs and infection.

The history of antiseptic solution and the discovery of alcohol goes back to the ninth century by a Persian chemist/physician named Dr. Razi. (842-932 AD)

Razi and Avicenna (980-1037) both used alcohol for wound irrigation. Razi made many ointments, alcohol based for local use and medical purposes. Pasteur used heat to sterilize the wounds, Lister sprayed carbolic acid over the wound during the operation to kill the germs called "disease dust."

Sir Alexander Fleming (1881-1955)

He was a British bacteriologist who discovered penicillin and he shared a 1945 Nobel Prize for his achievement. By D-Day 1944, Fleming had produced enough penicillin to treat every one of the forty thousand soldiers wounded in Normandy. The production of the penicillin became a wartime priority for the United States with the bombing of Pearl Harbor in Hawaii.

A woman dying in New Haven, Connecticut, was treated with penicillin and it was finally proven to be effective once and for all. This drug went into production in 1942. This same drug was used during World War II to treat Mr. Churchill who suffered from pneumonia. Fleming had saved Mr.Churchill's life for the second time. The first time, Alexander Fleming saved Mr. Churchill when he was younger.

In 1929, Alexander Fleming reported in the British Journal of Experimental Pathology his observations on the antibacterial action of penicillium with the suggestion that the mold culture could be used to inhibit bacteria as help in obtaining their cultural isolation. Whatever Fleming may have thought of the eventual usefulness of what he called penicillin, there was virtually no further research until H. Florey and E. Chain in England in 1941 after extensive studies convinced them that penicillin had great therapeutic potential. The only difficulty was that penicillin could not be made in quantity in the laboratory. This was solved by cooperation with the United States Government and the pharmaceutical manufactures within two years after Florey and Chain had transferred their work to America.

Ivan Petrovich Pavlov (1849-1936)

This Russian physiologist is best known for discovering the condition response. He won the 1904 Nobel Prize for research on the digestion (Pavlovian condition reflex. After having studied at the Ludwig and Heidenhain laboratories in Germany, he became Professor of Pharmacology, and later Professor of Physiology at the military medical academy in Russia. He did a detail investigation of the liver, heart, pancreas, and the alimentary tract. His most influential work was done on the condition reflux.

Jonnas Edward Salk (1915-1995)

He was an American microbiologist, who developed the first effective killed-virus vaccine against polio. Salk was born in New York in 1915 and wanted to be a lawyer, but thank God he changed his mind.

During the early 1950s, polio had paralyzed or killed about 40,000 Americans each year. The head of the American Medical Association, Dwight Murry, remarked Salk's vaccine was "one of the greatest events in the history of mankind. Salk wrote a number of books about the future of mankind, survival of the wisest, and man unfolds. He received numerous honors including the Novel Prize, the Congressional Gold Medal, and the Presidential Medal of Freedom. He established the Salk Institute for biological studies in La Jolla, California in April 12, 1955. President Dwight D. Eisenhower once commented to Salk regarding the creation of the polio vaccine, "I have no words to thank you. I am very, very happy." Salk was a medical hero equal to Louis Pateur.

Zakariya Razi (842-932 AD)

A physician, philospher, and an author of 237 books. Abu-Bakr Mohammed Ibn Zakariya Razi (Rasie), known in the Western world as Rhazes. He was born in the city of Ray about twenty miles south of Tehran, in Perse-Persia. His father was a goldsmith. Razi studied physics and chemistry during his early life and later became a famous chemist of his time. He later turned his attention to study of medicine.

Although small pox has existed since antiquity, the first graphic description of small pox and its differentiation from measles was written in 910 by Razi in the Arabic language - the language used for scholarly work of the time. Thirty-six of his books deal with science and medicine. He produced medical alcohol and used it for antiseptic purposes and many ointments with copper sulfate, iron sulfate, borax, alcohol bases and other mercurial ointments. Razi treated the poor free of charge as he is regarded as the "father of pediatrics." He wrote on the topic of embryology and spinal injury in a twenty four volume encyclopedia dealing with different aspects of medicine. Razi spent most of his life in Persia where he was born, later as a chief of the hospital in Ray.

Razi was chosen to be Chief Physician in Motazedi Hospital in Baghdad.

"Al-Hawi," is his most famous book and was first translated into Latin in 1227-1279, as well as multiple other languages. His elegant works were the standard of many countries around the world. "Kitab Al- Mansouri" (Mansour was the ruler of the city of Ray), the second most popular book relates to topics of surgery and medicine.

You can find at Princeton University in New Jersey, a stain glass window in the chapel on campus with the writing of Razi's, the beautiful masterpiece is entitled "Al-Hawy." The stain glass was designed by Charles Conning of Boston and donated to the church in memory of Dr. Paul H. Ludington. A portion of Razi's references, books, and journals were printed in London in 1848 for the Sydenham Society of England. The original version, portrayer of smallpox, was by Abas M. Behbehani, PhD. And a recent reprint was in JAMA (Journal of American Medical Association) December 14, 1984. The Princeton University library has excellent reference information about Razi and I had the pleasure of reviewing some of the related documents and papers during a recent visit.

Ibu Sina Avicenna, Abu Ali Sina Avicenna (980-1037)

Avicenna was born near Bukkhara, Persia. He was a well-respected and equal to Galen as a philosopher and physician. He wrote about a hundred books and many were later translated in Europe. Canon of Medicine (law of medicine and surgery) was the most famous book. Practitioners based their medical ideas and procedures from his book until the mid seventeenth century.

Medical curriculum including those in the British Isle, were based on Avicenna's writings as well. His scientific works and papers were written in Arabic but his poetry was written in his native "Farsi" Persian language. Ibn Sina was called the Prince of Physicians. Sir William Osler, a great physician himself, regarded Avicenna as one of the greatest names in the history of medicine.

Avicenna's textbook "Canon of Medicine" is a Greek word, which stands for the standard contains a million words in five books. These are general principles of medical practice, simple drugs, local diseases, general disease and compound medicines. He discusses extensively on breast cancer surgery, subjects including anatomy, hygiene, medicine, surgery, diagnosis, treatment, pharmacology, and sports medicine. There are extensive discussions on the prevention of diseases and psychology. Avicenna books were translated into Latin around 1175 and later into other languages.

Like his predecessor, Razi, Avicenna used alcohol as an antiseptic for irrigation of wounds. In the "Canon of Medicine", Avicenna describes 15 types of body pain: compressing, dull, boring, corrosive, heavy, irritant, incisive, itching, throbbing, fatigue, and relaxing. He also described in detail the use of analgesic drugs from herbs, seeds, roots, and barks containing alkaloids as well as hypnotic to the most powerful narcotics of opium. He goes into further detail about the effects and side effects of these medications. You can refer to the textbook for more detailed information on cardio-vascular disease, diabetes, urology, etc. Throughout the history of medicine from ancient Chinese and Hindu writings through the age of Hippocrates and Galen, the contribution of Razi and Avicenna are legacies that are still alive in the medical world today.

Louis Pasteur (1822-1895)

He firmly established the germ theory of diseases. A French chemist who founded modern microbiology, modern pasteurization, and developed a vaccine for anthrax. In 1885, a young boy named Joseph Meister, who had been bitten by a rabid dog was brought to him. Pasteur first consulted two physicians who agreed that the boy's outlook was hopeless. Pasteur injected untested anti-rabies inoculation into the boy and he recovered. That unthinkable experiment became the foundation of modern vaccinations.

In 1988, a grateful France founded the Pasteur Institute. Pasteur's seventieth birthday was the occasion of a national holiday. At the end of the celebration in Sorbonne, Pasteur was too weak to speak to the delegates who had gathered from around the world. His address, was read by his son who concluded; "Gentleman you bring me the greatest happiness that can be experienced by a man whose invincible belief is that science and peace will triumph over ignorance and war... Have faith that in the long run... the future will belong not to the conquerors but to the saviors of mankind"

Robert Koch (1843-1910)

He was born in Germany. While practicing as a country physician he spent his spare moments studying microorganism. By the time of his death, he had revolutionized bacteriology and had established the sporulation and pathogenic characters of the anthrax bacillus, developed and refined the techniques of culturing bacteria, advanced the methods of steam sterilization, and discovered the causes of many diseases. This included wound infections, cholera, Egyptian ophthalmia, and sleeping sickness. He also introduced effective preventive measures in typhoid fever, the plague, malaria and other diseases.

Certainly, his two most influential contributions were the isolation of the tubercle bacillus (the cause of tuberculosis) and the establishment of the essential steps ("Koch Postules") required proof that an organism was the cause of the disease. Robert Koch won in Geneva, the Nobel Prize for his discoveries in relation to tuberculosis.

Florence Nightingale (1820-1910)

She was known as "the lady with the lamp." She was born on May 20, 1820 in Florence, Italy. She was a British nurse who organized and directed a unit of field nurses during the Crimean War and was considered the founder of modern nursing. Ms. Nightingale set the standards for practices and procedures and developed the nursing profession. She was responsible for the establishment of the first military medical school. In civilian life, she was the moving spirit and architectural mind behind the reconstruction of the Saint Thomas's Hospital of England.

William Stewart Halsted (1852-1922)

He was a great teacher and master surgeon at John Hopkins in Baltimore, Maryland, with a vast vision. He was famous for the surgical performance of a radical mastectomy for breast cancer. Suffice to say, that the first historical reference to breast cancer had been recorded about three thousand BC on surgical papyrus. Halsted led the most prestigious program of surgery in the nineteenth century.

An interesting Halsted story concerned his introduction of rubber gloves in surgery as a response to the dermatitis on the scrub nurse hands, who he respected as "a very efficient woman." Dermatitis was due to the antiseptic carbolic acid spray that was used during that time. Dr. Halsted used x-ray for diagnosis and he used radiotherapy and also hormone manipulation after surgery for breast cancer.

Secret Memories

In conclusion, each life affects another's. We may not always realize that everything we do affects not only our lives but touches others too. For a moment of thoughtfulness that you show someone, your care can create a ray of sunshine or positive energy for both of you to share.

As a thirteenth century Persian Poet, Sadi said,
>*I had in mind when I reached to the garden*
>*to bring you a basket of flowers.*
>*But when I reached there*
>*the smell of roses and jasmine*
>*and the musical sound of nightingales*
>*made me so unconscious*
>*that I forgot what I came for.*

Future

*Man has two sets of eyes, one set to see
Another is eternal and Divine.*
Book of Angels

As time goes on, the mind of man will become more electronic, but since the power of spirituality and great faiths are connecting bridges not obstacles. Yet the solutions to the most human problems are internal and not external. It is better to have a well balance life, physically, mentally, and spiritually which is essential for a healthy, happy, loving, and peaceful life.

The gift of vision with love and positive energy will encourage the thought of mankind towards self healing and a helping hand with compassion will be beneficial to self and others. Keep the furnace of *"hope"* in your heart and soul alive and practice the doctrines of "Good thought, good words and good deeds," on a daily basis and peace of mind will follow.

The primary goal today for treating the people with high risk for developing cancer should be directed toward education and prevention rather than wait and see. The highly complex and challenging advances in human genetics has potential for improvement in the health of people with family histories of cancer as well as non malignant conditions. Preventative medicine and human genome projects are beneficial for all segments of the United States population; and number one priority should be the quality of life with preservation of life. Researchers are contemplating to isolate more specific medications for a specific condition such as cancer. For anxiety and pain management, first do no harm. Alternative therapies at certain times are as effective as man made drugs.

For me, I look beyond the clouds and I say; "as long as the sky is blue, the sun is shining and the beautiful flowers are smiling, I smile too." You smile too...

Thank you God.
Mir

About the Author

Mahmood Mir, M.D., F.A.C.S.

- Born in Shiraz, Iran, State of Fars, and raised in Tehran
- Graduated from Pahlavi University, Iran, Medical and Surgical Training in Chicago, Illinois, and Fellowship at Queens Central Hospital in New York City, New York
- Board Certified Surgeon by American Board of Surgery
- Teaching Positions at Cancer Institute, Tehran, and VA Medical Center, Dayton, Ohio
- Member of the American College of Surgeons and Medical Delegate for American Cancer Society of Ohio.
- Practiced surgery over 20 years in Ohio and at the present time resides in Southern California

Research & Publications
Lifestyle, Diet and Cancer
Carcinoma of the Colon & Rectum
Echionoccus Cysts of the Liver and Lung
Carotid Body Tumor
Perforated Esophagus with Diaphragmatic Patch Graft
Septicemia and Septic Shock
Carcinoma of the Prostate Presenting as Obstruction Carcinoma of the Rectum
Multiple Cancer Syndrome